TIME FOR GOD

TIME FOR GOD

A guide to mental prayer

Jacques Philippe

Translated by Helena Scott

 Scepter

Originally published as *Du Temps pour Dieu*
Copyright © 1992, Editions des Beatitudes, S.O.C.
Burtin, France

English translation copyright © 2008
Scepter Publishers, Inc.
P.O. Box 1391, New Rochelle, N.Y. 10802
www.scepterpublishers.org
All rights reserved.

ISBN 978–1–59417-066–9

CONTENTS

IV. Material conditions for mental prayer

V. Some methods of mental prayer

APPENDICES

INTRODUCTION

In the Western Catholic tradition the term "prayer" covers many different activities. The following pages mainly concentrate on mental prayer: prayer that consists of facing God in solitude and silence for a time in order to enter into intimate, loving communion with him. Practicing this kind of prayer regularly is considered by all spiritual masters to be a privileged, indispensable path that gives access to genuine Christian life—a path to knowing and loving God that empowers us to respond to his call to holiness addressed to each individual.

It is a wonderful fact that many people today are thirsty for God and feel a desire for that sort of intense, personal prayer life; they would like to be able to spend time praying as a regular thing. But they encounter obstacles that prevent them from following the path seriously, and especially from persevering on it. Sometimes they don't receive the encouragement needed to make up their minds to begin, or else they feel helpless because they simply don't know how to start. Sometimes, after repeated attempts, they become discouraged by the difficulties and abandon the regular practice of mental prayer. It's a pity, because perseverance in mental prayer, according to the unanimous testimony of all the saints, is the narrow gate that opens the Kingdom of Heaven to us; it is the only way for us to receive the gifts which "no eye has seen, nor ear heard, nor the heart of man conceived, what God has prepared for those who love him" (1 Cor 2:9). Mental prayer is the source of true happiness. Whoever practices it faithfully will not fail to "taste and see that the Lord is good" (Ps 34). Those who pray will find the living water that Jesus promised: "Whoever drinks of the water that I shall give him will never thirst" (Jn 4:14).

Convinced of this truth as I am, my aim in this book is to provide advice and orientation and do that as simply and specifically as possible. I hope this may help everyone who has good will and a desire for mental prayer to set out and persevere on the path of prayer, without being overcome by the inevitable difficulties.

There are plenty of books about mental prayer. The great contemplatives have spoken about it much better than I can, and I will quote them frequently. Nevertheless, it seems to me that today's believers need a presentation of the Church's traditional teaching that is simple and easily accessible, adapted to today's outlook and expressed in today's language. Such a presentation also needs to take account of the pedagogy that God in his wisdom is using today to lead souls to holiness; it is not always the same as in past centuries. These, then, are the reasons which moved me to write this book.

I Mental prayer is not a technique but a grace

1. *Mental prayer is not a kind of Christian yoga*

To persevere in a life of prayer we obviously need to avoid heading down the wrong road at the start. Thus we need to determine what is specific to Christian prayer—what distinguishes it from other activities of the spirit. This is all the more important since we may react against the materialistic culture around us by developing a sort of thirst for the absolute, for mysticism and communion with the unseen. Such is a good in itself, but it can easily lead one to deceptive and even harmful experiences.

The first, basic truth, without which we will not get very far, is that the life of prayer (or contemplative prayer, to use a different name for the same thing), is not the result of a technique, but a gift we receive. St. Jane Frances de Chantal used to say, "The best method of prayer is not to have one, because prayer is not obtained by artifice"—by technique, we would say today—"but by grace." There is no "method" of praying, in the sense of a set of instructions or procedures that we merely have to apply in order to pray well. Though true contemplative prayer is a gift that God gives freely, we do need to understand how to receive it.

This point needs to be stressed for several reasons. First, of course, Eastern meditation methods—yoga, Zen, etc. —are widely known in today's world. Moreover, the modern mindset wants to reduce everything to a technique. And third, the human mind is forever tempted to try to make life, including spiritual life, into something to be manipulated at will. For all these reasons we often have, consciously or unconsciously, a false image of contemplative prayer as a sort of Christian yoga. We imagine that set procedures of mental concentration and recollection, appropriate breathing techniques, prescribed physical positions, the repetition of certain formulas, and so on should cause us to progress in mental prayer. When thoroughly mastered through practice, we believe, these things should enable one to attain a higher state of consciousness. But this view gives a completely false picture of mental prayer and the mystical life in Christianity.

It is false because it leads us to cling to methods that depend ultimately on human effort, whereas in fact, as Christianity sees it, everything is grace, a free gift from God. True, there may be a certain resemblance between Eastern ascetics or "holy men" and Christian contemplatives, but the resemblance is superficial. At bottom they inhabit very different, even incompatible, realms.[1]

[1] To go deeper into this question, see the book *Des bords du Gange aux rives du Jourdain*, by Hans Urs von Balthasar (Paris: Editions Saint-Paul, 1983).

Note: There is a further essential difference between Christian spirituality and the spiritual methods derived from the wisdom of the non-Christian East. In Eastern-inspired spiritualities the goal of the spiritual journey is very often

The essential difference has been pointed out. On the one hand, it all comes down to technique, an activity depending essentially on human beings and their capabilities. This is so even when such systems claim to invoke special capabilities, left unused by ordinary mortals, which the "meditation technique" in question proposes to reveal and develop. On the other hand, by contrast, it is a matter of God giving himself freely to someone. Even if, as we shall see, there is room for a certain amount of initiative and activity on the human side, the whole edifice of the life of prayer is built on God's initiative and his grace. We must never lose sight of this fact, for one of the permanent and sometimes subtle temptations of the spiritual life is to rely on our efforts and not on God's freely given mercy.

There are many very important consequences to what has just been said. Let's look more closely at a few.

---

either making the *self* absolute, or a sort of absorption of the self into the All, ending suffering by ending desire and losing individuality. In Christianity, however, the ultimate goal of contemplative prayer is profoundly different: to be divinized through union with God in a face-to-face encounter, a loving union of person with person. This union is deep, but it preserves the distinction between persons, so that there can be a true reciprocal giving of the self in love.

It is also important to be very much on guard against the widespread currents that go under the name "New Age." This is a sort of syncretism or mixture of astrology, reincarnation, oriental modes of thought, and so on. It is a modern form of gnosis that completely denies the mystery of the Incarnation and reflects an illusory desire for self-realization without grace (exactly the opposite of what is proposed in this book). The approach is ultimately very selfish, since other persons are never considered according to their own value but only as instruments to "my" self-realization. Here is a world with no true relationships to other people, no "otherness," and hence no love.

2. *Some immediate consequences*

The first consequence is that, even though methods or exercises can be helpful in mental prayer, we should not attach too much importance to them, much less imagine that everything depends on them. To do that would mean centering the life of prayer on ourselves instead of God, and that is just the mistake we must avoid. Nor should we imagine that all we need is a bit of practice, or learning certain "tricks," and then all our difficulties, distractions, etc., in prayer will vanish. The profound logic of growth and progress in the spiritual life belongs to a totally different order. And that is just as well, for if the edifice of prayer had to be built up on our efforts we wouldn't get very far. St. Teresa of Avila says "the whole edifice of prayer is founded upon humility"—on the conviction that of ourselves we can do nothing, and it is God, and he alone, who can produce good in our souls. Pride may make this idea distasteful to us, but in fact it is enormously liberating. God, who loves us, will carry us infinitely further and higher than we could ever get on our own steam.

The fundamental principle stated above has another liberating consequence. With any technique, there are always some people who have a gift for it, and others who don't. If prayer were a matter of technique, the same would be true: some people would be capable of contemplative prayer and others would not. Yes, some people do find it easier than others to be recollected and to dwell on lofty considerations. But it doesn't matter. Every single person, in accordance with his or her own personality, his or her own gifts and weaknesses, can have a deep prayer life by corresponding faithfully to God's grace. The call to prayer, to the mystical life, to union with God in prayer, is as universal as the call to holiness. The two things, prayer and holiness, are intimately linked, and absolutely nobody is excluded. Jesus is speaking not to a chosen elite but to all people without exception when he says, "Pray at all times" (Lk 21: 36), and "When you pray, go into your room and shut the door and pray to your Father who is in secret; and your Father who sees in secret will reward you" (Mt 6: 6).

There is another consequence, one fundamental to the plan of this book. If the life of prayer is not a technique to be mastered but a grace to be received, a gift from God, then talk about prayer should not focus on describing methods or giving instructions, but on explaining the necessary conditions for receiving the gift. These conditions are certain inner attitudes, certain dispositions of the heart. What ensures progress in the life of prayer, what makes it fruitful, is not so much how we pray as our inner dispositions in beginning and continuing it. Our principal task is to try to acquire, keep, and deepen those dispositions of the heart. God will do the rest.

Now let us look at the most important of these dispositions.

3. *Faith and trust as the basis for mental prayer*

The first and most fundamental disposition is an attitude of faith. The life of prayer includes struggle, and the essential weapon for this struggle is faith.

Faith is the capacity of believers to act not according to impressions, preconceived ideas, or notions borrowed from other people, but according to what they are told by the Word of God, who cannot lie. Understood in this way, the virtue of faith is the basis for all mental prayer. It is activated in different ways.

FAITH IN GOD'S PRESENCE   In starting to pray, alone, facing God, in our room, or in an oratory before the Blessed Sacrament, we must believe with our whole heart that God is present. Regardless of what we may or may not feel, the preparation we have or haven't made, how good we are or aren't at stringing beautiful thoughts together— regardless of our whole inner state—God is there, with us, looking at us and loving us. He is not there because we deserve him or feel his presence, but because he gave his promise: "Go into your room, shut the door, and pray to your Father who *is* there in secret . . ." (Mt 6:6).

Even if we are arid or wretched, or feel that God is absent or even has abandoned us, we should never let ourselves doubt God's loving, welcoming presence to someone who prays to him. "Him who comes to me, I will not cast out" (Jn 6:37). God is there long before we put ourselves in his presence. It is he who invites us to come and meet him—he, our Father, who is waiting for us and who seeks to enter into communion with us with an urgency far surpassing ours. God desires us infinitely more than we desire him.

FAITH THAT ALL ARE CALLED TO MEET GOD IN PRAYER, AND THAT GOD GIVES THE GRACE WE NEED FOR THIS MEET-ING   Whatever difficulties, resistance, or objections we may have, we must believe firmly that all people without exception, wise and ignorant, just and sinners, well-balanced and deeply wounded, are called to an authentic life of prayer in which God will communicate himself to us. And since it is God who calls us, and he is just, he will give everyone the graces needed to persevere in mental prayer and make the life of prayer a deep, marvelous experience of communion with his inner life. The life of prayer is not reserved for a religious elite: it is for everyone. The widely held notion that "it isn't for me— it's for other people, who are holier or better than I am," is contrary to the Gospel. Never mind the difficulties and weaknesses. God will give the strength we need.

FAITH IN THE FRUITFULNESS OF THE LIFE OF PRAYER   The life of prayer is the source of infinite riches. It transforms us within, sanctifies us, heals us, helps us to know and love God, makes us fervent and generous in love of neighbor. Provided they persevere, those who commit themselves to a life of prayer can be absolutely sure of receiving all this and more. Although we may sometimes have the opposite impression—that our prayer life is sterile, that we are stumbling, that praying doesn't change anything— even though we think we can't see the hoped-for results in our lives, we must not be discouraged. God will keep his promise: "Ask, and it will be given you; seek, and you will find; knock, and it will be opened to you" (Lk 11:9-10). All those who persevere in that trust will receive infinitely more than they dared to ask or hope for: not because they deserve it, but because God has promised.

People are often tempted to give up mental prayer because they don't see the results as soon as they would like. This temptation should be rejected immediately by making an act of faith in God's promise, which will be fulfilled when the time is right. "Be patient, therefore, brethren, until the coming of the Lord. Behold, the farmer waits for the precious fruits of the earth, being patient over it until it receives the early and the late rain. You also must be patient. Establish your hearts, for the coming of the Lord is at hand" (Jas 5:7-8).

4. *Fidelity and perseverance*

This leads to a very important practical conclusion.

Someone who sets out on a life of prayer should aim in the first place at *fidelity*. What matters is not whether our mental prayer is beautiful, or whether it works, or whether it is enriched by deep thoughts and feelings, but whether it is persevering and faithful. Our first concern, if I may put it that way, should be faithfulness in praying, not the quality of our prayer. The quality will come from fidelity. Time spent faithfully every day in mental prayer that is poor, arid, distracted, and relatively short is worth more, and will be infinitely more fruitful for our progress, than long, ardent spells of mental prayer from time to time, when circumstances make it easy. After that first decision to take the prayer life seriously, the first battle we must fight is the battle to be faithful to our times of mental prayer, come what may, according to a definite plan we have established. It is not an easy battle. Knowing how much is at stake, the devil wants at all costs to keep us from being faithful to mental prayer. He knows that a person who is faithful to mental prayer has escaped from him, or at least is sure of escaping in the end. He therefore does everything he can to prevent us from being faithful. We shall return to this point later.

What is important here is that mental prayer that is of poor quality but regular and faithful, is worth more than prayer that is sublime but only now and then. It is faithfulness alone that enables the life of prayer to bear wonderful fruit.

Mental prayer is basically no more than an exercise in loving God. But there is no true love without fidelity. How could we claim to love God if we failed to keep the appointments we make with him for mental prayer?

5. *Purity of intention*

Besides faith and the fidelity which is its practical expression, another basic inner attitude for anyone who wants to persevere in mental prayer is purity of intention. Jesus tells us, "Blessed are the pure in heart, for they shall see God" (Mt 5: 8). In Gospel terms, "the pure in heart" are not people without sin who never have anything to reproach themselves for, but those who are inspired in all they do by a sincere intention of forgetting themselves in order to please God, living not for themselves but for him. This is an indispensable condition for mental prayer. We pray not to find self-fulfillment or self-satisfaction, but to please God. Without that, we will not be able to persevere. Those who seek themselves and their own satisfaction will quickly drop mental prayer when it becomes difficult or dry and does not please and gratify them as they expected. Genuine love is pure love that does not seek its own interests but has as its single aim giving joy to the loved person. We should not pray for the sake of the satisfactions or benefits we derive (even if they are immense) but mainly to please God, because he asks us to.

Purity of intention like that is demanding, but also enormously liberating and satisfying. Those who seek themselves will quickly become discouraged and worried when their mental prayer "doesn't work." Those who love God purely won't be troubled when that happens. If prayer is difficult and they do not get satisfaction from it, they don't have a fit; they console themselves with the thought that what matters is to give their time freely to God, simply for *his* satisfaction, *his* joy.

At this point someone might object, "It would certainly be great to love God as purely as that—but who can do it?" The purity of intention just described is indispensable, but, unsurprisingly, there is no way of perfectly acquiring it at the very start of the spiritual life. We are asked only to aim for it consciously and practice it as well as we can in times of dryness when it's needed. All these who undertake a spiritual journey obviously seek themselves in part at the same time they seek God. But it doesn't matter as long as we never cease to aspire to an ever purer love for God.

The point is worth making in order to call attention to a trap that the devil, the Accuser, frequently uses to worry and discourage us. He makes it clear to us how imperfect and weak our love for God still is—how much self-seeking remains in our spiritual life.

Above all, this realization that we still seek ourselves in prayer must not upset us. We should tell God, very simply, that we want to love him with a pure, disinterested love, and then abandon ourselves totally and trustingly to him. He will purify us. Hoping to achieve that purity by our own strength, wanting to decide for ourselves what is pure and impure in us—to uproot the weeds prematurely, as it were—and thereby falling into mere presumption; we would risk uprooting the good wheat too (see Mt

13: 20-34). Let God's grace act. Be content to persevere in trust. Patiently endure the times of aridity that God will certainly send to purify our love for him.

Another temptation can also sometimes arise. Since purity of intention consists of seeking and pleasing God instead of oneself, the devil sometimes tries to discourage us with the following argument. "How can you imagine your prayer could ever please God, when you are so full of faults!" The reply is a truth at the heart of the Gospel— a truth that the Holy Spirit moved St. Thérèse of Lisieux to remind us of: people do not please God primarily by their virtues and merits, but above all by their limitless trust in his mercy. We shall come back to this point.

6. *Humility and poverty of heart*

Recall St. Teresa of Avila's words, "The whole edifice of prayer is founded upon humility." Scripture says that "God opposes the proud, but gives grace to the humble" (1 Pet 5: 5).

Humility, then, is one of the basic attitudes of the heart without which perseverance in mental prayer is impossible.

Humility lies in peaceful acceptance of one's own radical poverty, which leads people to place all their trust in God. Humble people, for whom God is everything, are happy to accept the fact that they are nothing. They don't carry on about their wretchedness: they consider it a stroke of luck, since it gives God the chance to show how merciful he is.

Without humility we cannot persevere in mental prayer. In fact, doing mental prayer necessarily means experiencing our poverty, being stripped of everything, feeling naked. In other kinds of prayer and spiritual activities there is always something to support us: a certain knowledge of how to do these things correctly, the sense of doing something useful, and so on. Even in community prayer, we can rely on the others. But in solitude and silence before God, we find ourselves unsupported, alone with the reality of our self and our poverty. Of course, it is very difficult for us to accept the fact that we are so poor; that is why people naturally tend to avoid silence. And in mental prayer the experience of poverty can't be avoided. True, we may often experience the sweetness and tenderness of God; but just as often we shall find our own wretchedness: our inability to pray, our distractions, the wounds of our memory and imagination, the recollection of our faults and failures, worries for the future, etc. This is why people have no difficulty discovering a thousand excuses for avoiding that state of inaction before God, that lays bare their radical nothingness; ultimately, they refuse to be poor and weak.

Yet it is precisely that trusting, joyful acceptance of weakness that is the source of all spiritual riches: "Blessed are the poor in spirit, for theirs is the Kingdom of Heaven" (Mt 5: 3).

Humble people persevere in the life of prayer without presumption and without relying on themselves. They don't consider anything as their due, don't consider themselves able to do anything by their own strength, aren't surprised to find that they have difficulties, weaknesses, and constant falls, but put up with all these peacefully, without making much of them, because they place all their hope in God and are certain that they will obtain from God's mercy all that they are powerless to do or merit for themselves.

Humble people are never discouraged because they trust not in themselves but in God. Ultimately, that is what really matters. "It is discouragement that causes souls to be lost," says Father Libermann. True humility and trust always go hand-in-hand.

For example, we must never let ourselves become discouraged over our lukewarmness or the realization of how little we love God. Beginners in the spiritual life, on reading the lives of saints or their writings, may sometimes feel downhearted in the face of the burning expressions of love for God they find there, so far beyond anything they themselves feel. They tell themselves they will never attain these heights. This is a very common temptation. Let us persevere in good will and trust: God himself will give us the love with which we can love him. Strong, burning love for God does not come naturally. It is infused in our hearts by the Holy Spirit, who will be given to us if we ask for him with the persistence of the widow in the Gospel. It is not always those who feel the most fervent at the start who go furthest in the spiritual life—far from it, in fact!

7. *Determination to persevere*

It should be clear by now that the main battle in mental prayer is perseverance. God will give us the grace to persevere if we ask him for it trustingly and are firmly resolved to do whatever is up to us.

We need lots of determination, especially at the beginning. St. Teresa of Avila stresses this:

> Let us now return to those who wish to travel on this road, and will not halt until they reach their goal, which is the place where they can drink of this water of life. As I say, it is most important—all-important, indeed—that they should begin well by making an earnest and most determined resolve not to halt until they reach their goal, whatever may come, whatever may happen to them, however hard they may have to labor, whoever may complain of them, whether they reach their goal or die on the road or have no heart to confront the trials which they meet, whether the very world dissolves before them.[2]

Now we turn to some considerations meant to strengthen that determination and uncover the traps, false arguments, or temptations that may undermine it.

[2] St. Teresa of Avila, *Way of Perfection*, trans. E. Allison Peers (Sheed & Ward, 1946), chap. 21.

WITHOUT A LIFE OF PRAYER THERE IS NO HOLINESS   First, we need to be convinced of the vital importance of mental prayer. "He who avoids prayer is avoiding everything that is good," said St. John of the Cross. All the saints have spent time praying. Those who were most involved in the service of their neighbor were also contemplatives. St. Vincent de Paul began each day with two or three hours of mental prayer and meditation.

There is no spiritual progress without contemplative prayer. Even though we may have had a powerful conversion experience, felt great fervor, and received immense graces, without fidelity to mental prayer our Christian life will soon reach a plateau and stall there. This is because without mental prayer we cannot receive all the help from God that we need to be transformed and sanctified in depth. The testimony of the saints is unanimous on this point.

Now, some people might object that sanctifying grace also—indeed, mainly—comes to us through the sacraments. Mass is in itself more important than mental prayer. This is true, but without a life of prayer even the sacraments will have only a limited effect. Yes, they will give us grace, but that grace will remain unfruitful in part because the "good soil" it needs is missing. Why, for instance, are so many people who receive Communion frequently not more holy? The reason often is that they do not have a life of prayer. The Blessed Eucharist does not bring all the fruits of inner healing and sanctification that it should, because it is not being received with an attitude of faith, love, adoration, and total receptivity—an attitude that can only be created by fidelity to mental prayer. The same is true of the other sacraments.

If someone, even someone very devout and committed, has not made a habit of mental prayer, something will always be lacking for the growth of his or her spiritual life. People like this will not find true inner peace but will always be subject to anxiety, and there will always be something too merely human in what they do: attachment to their own will, traces of vanity, self-seeking, ambition, narrow-mindedness, and so on. There can be no deep, radical purification of the heart without the practice of mental prayer. Otherwise, our wisdom and prudence will always remain on the human plane, and we will never reach true inner freedom. Otherwise, we cannot know God's mercy from the inside, nor can we bring other people to know it. Our judgment will remain narrow and uncertain and we will be unable really and truly to enter upon the paths of God, which are very different from what many people—even committed Christians—imagine.

For example, some people have a wonderful experience of conversion in Charismatic Renewal. The outpouring of the Spirit is a luminous, overwhelming encounter with God. But after a few months or years they cease making progress and lose their spiritual vitality. Why? Because God has withdrawn his hand from them?

Certainly not. "The gifts of God are irrevocable" (Rom 11:29). It is because they did not learn to remain permanently open to his grace by making the experience of the Renewal bear fruit in a life of prayer.

THE PROBLEM OF NOT ENOUGH TIME   "I'd really like to do mental prayer, but I don't have the time." How often this has been said! And in a hyperactive world like our own, the difficulty is a real one and should not be underestimated.

But time is not always the real problem. That real problem is knowing what really matters in life. As a contemporary author remarked, no one yet has starved to death because they didn't have the time to eat. We always find (or rather take!) the time to do what really matters to us. Before saying we don't have time for mental prayer, let's begin by reviewing our hierarchy of values, to see what our real priorities are.

One of the great crises of our day is that people are no longer capable of finding time for one another, time to be with one another. Here is something that causes many deep wounds. So many children are enclosed within themselves, disillusioned and damaged, because their parents never learned to spend time with them, with nothing else to do except be with their child. They look after the child, but they are always doing something else or are preoccupied, never entirely there, never totally available. And the child senses this and suffers. In learning to give time to God, we will certainly become more able to find time to be there for one another. Our attentiveness to God will teach us to be attentive to others.

Regarding this problem of time, we should make an act of faith in Jesus' promise: "There is no one who has left house or brothers or sisters or mother or father or children or land, for my sake and for the gospel, who will not receive a hundredfold now in this time!" (Mk 10: 29). It is legitimate to apply this to chronological time as well: whoever gives up a quarter of an hour of television in order to pray will receive a hundredfold in this life—the time will be returned to them a hundredfold, not in quantity but in quality. Mental prayer will give one the grace to live out every moment of life in a much more fruitful way.

TIME GIVEN TO GOD IS NOT TIME STOLEN FROM OTHER PEOPLE   To persevere in mental prayer, then, we need to set aside certain mistaken feelings of guilt arising from a false notion of charity, and be thoroughly convinced that time given to God is never time stolen from other people who need our love and our presence. On the contrary, fidelity in being present to God guarantees the capacity to be present to others and love them truly. Experience proves this: the love of prayerful souls is the most attentive, delicate, disinterested, sensitive to other people's suffering, and capable of consoling and comforting. Mental prayer makes us better people, and those who are close to us won't complain about that!

Many untrue things have been said about the connection between a life of prayer and charity towards one's neighbor, and these untruths have turned Christians away from contemplative prayer, with dire consequences. A lot could be said on this score. Here is a passage from St. John of the Cross that can straighten out people's thinking on this subject and vindicate those Christians who, quite legitimately, wish to dedicate much time to prayer.

> Let those who are fully taken up with activity, who imagine they can move the world by their preaching and their other external works, reflect here for a moment; they will easily understand that they would be much more useful to the Church, and more pleasing to the Lord, not to mention the good example they would set around them, if they dedicated half their time to mental prayer, even though they may not be as advanced as the soul described here. If they did, they would accomplish a greater good by one single work, and with much less effort, than they now accomplish by the thousand works on which they spend their lives. Mental prayer would merit them this grace, and would obtain for them the spiritual strength which they need in order to produce such fruits. Without it, everything is merely noise; it is the hammer which falls on the anvil and wakes all the echoes in its surroundings. Such people do little more than nothing, sometimes absolutely nothing, or even do harm. God preserve us, in fact, from souls like that, if they begin to be puffed up with pride! Vain would be all the appearances in their favor; the truth is that they would

do nothing, because undoubtedly no good work can be accomplished without the virtue of God. Oh how many things could be written on this subject, if this were the place to do so![3]

IS IT SUFFICIENT TO PRAY WHILE WE WORK? People will tell you, "I don't have time to do mental prayer; but in the middle of my activities, doing the housework, and so on, I try to think about our Lord as much as possible. I offer up my work, and I figure that is prayer enough."

This is not all wrong. A man or woman may very well be in a state of close union with God in the middle of a busy life, so that this union constitutes their life of prayer, without their needing to do more. God our Lord may grant this grace to people, especially if it is absolutely impossible for them to do anything different. What is more, it is obviously highly recommended that we turn to God as often as we can in the middle of our activities. And finally, work offered up and done for God really does become a kind of prayer.

But granting all that, we also need to be realistic. It isn't so easy to be in a state of union with God while being immersed in activities. Our natural tendency is to be completely absorbed in what we are doing. If we do not learn how to stop completely from time to time, how to make a space in which we do nothing except think about God, we will find it very difficult to remain in God's presence while

[3] *Spiritual Canticle B*, strophe 29.

working. To do that, we need a thorough re-education of our heart, and fidelity to mental prayer is the surest way to achieve it.

This is how it is with all interpersonal relationships. Someone who believes he loves his wife and children despite having a very active life, but who cannot find any time to be one hundred percent available to them, may be kidding himself. Without that free space, love will soon be stifled. Love expands and breathes in an atmosphere of free giving. We must be able to waste time for another person. We will gain great benefits from that "waste": it is one of the realities signified by the Gospel words "He who loses his life for my sake will find it" (Mt 10: 39).

If we make God our first concern, God will look after our affairs much better than we ever can. Let us acknowledge humbly that our natural tendency is to be too attached to our activities, to allow ourselves to be carried away by them till they fill our minds entirely. This won't change until we acquire the wise habit of abandoning all activities, even the most urgent and important ones, in order to give time freely to God.

THE TRAP OF FALSE SINCERITY   In an age as keen on freedom and authenticity as our own, an argument that comes up fairly often and may prevent people from being faithful to mental prayer goes like this:

"Prayer is terrific, but I only pray when I feel an inner need. . . . To start praying when I don't feel like it would be artificial, forced, even a sort of insincerity or hypocrisy. . . . I pray when I feel a spontaneous desire for it. . . ."

The answer is that if we wait until we feel the spontaneous desire for prayer, we may end up waiting until the end of our days. That desire for prayer is very beautiful, and also unreliable. There is another motive for going to meet God in mental prayer that is equally meaningful and far deeper and more constant: he invites us to. The Gospel tells us to "pray always" (Lk 18: 1). We should be guided by faith and not by our subjective mood.

The idea of freedom and authenticity expressed in the line of thought described above greatly suits people's tastes today; and it is very unsound. Real freedom does not mean being ruled by one's impulses from one moment to the next. Just the opposite. Being free means not being a slave to one's moods; it means being guided in a course of action by the fundamental choices one has made, choices one does not repudiate in the face of new circumstances.

Truth, not superficial inclination, is the guide to the authentic use of freedom. We must be humble enough to recognize how fickle we are. Someone who is wonderful today strikes us as unbearable tomorrow, thanks to a change in the weather or our mood. What we couldn't live without on Monday leaves us cold Tuesday. This kind of decision-making makes us the prisoners of our whims.

Nor should we deceive ourselves about authenticity.

Which is the most genuine, authentic love—the kind that changes from day to day according to mood, or the stable, faithful kind that never goes back on itself?

Faithfulness to mental prayer is a school of freedom. It is a school of truth in love, because it teaches us, little by little, no longer to place our relationship with God on the shaky, unstable basis of our own impressions, moods, or feelings, but on the solid foundation of faith—God's faithfulness, which is as firm as a rock. "Jesus Christ is the same yesterday and today, and forever" (Heb 13:8), for "His mercy is from generation to generation" (Lk 1:50). If we persevere, our relationships with other people, which are likewise superficial and changeable, will become more stable, more faithful, deeper, and hence happier.

One further point. Everyone wants to be able to act spontaneously, freely, without constraint. That is perfectly legitimate: human beings are not meant to be constantly at war with themselves, always doing violence to their nature. The need to battle with ourselves is a result of the inner divisions caused by sin. But our natural aspiration for freedom cannot be satisfied merely by giving free rein to spontaneous desire. That would be destructive, because our spontaneous desires are not always directed to what is good; they need to be deeply purified and healed. There is a wound in human nature—a lack of harmony, a split between what we spontaneously crave and what we were made for, between our feelings and the Will of God to which we must be faithful, and which is our true good.

Our yearning for freedom, then, can only be truly fulfilled insofar as we let ourselves be healed by God's grace. In that healing process, prayer plays a very important part. It also comes about— and we need to realize this—through trials and purifications, the "nights" whose meaning St. John of the Cross probed. Once this process of healing, which is the restoration of right order to our tendencies, has been accomplished, we become perfectly free; we naturally and spontaneously love and want what is in accordance with God's Will and our own good. Then, we can safely follow spontaneous tendencies, because they have been set right and brought into harmony with God's wisdom. Then we can do as "nature" bids us, because our nature will have been restored by grace. To be sure, our inner harmony will never be total in this present life, but only in heaven. Here below, we shall always have to fight against certain tendencies in us. But even in this life, people who practice mental prayer become increasingly capable of spontaneously loving and doing good, something that costs them much effort at the start. Thanks to the work of the Holy Spirit, virtue comes more easily and more naturally to them. "Where the Spirit of the Lord is, there is freedom," said St. Paul (2 Cor 3: 17).

THE TRAP OF FALSE HUMILITY We need to be on our guard against the false argument we have just considered, which sometimes takes a subtler form. St. Teresa of Avila almost fell into the trap and abandoned her mental prayer, and that would have meant an irreplaceable loss for the whole Church! One of her reasons for writing her *Autobiography* was to warn people against this trap, which the devil is very skillful at setting. It's this: someone who begins to do mental prayer soon realizes his or her own faults, infidelities, and areas not yet touched by grace. Then such a person may be tempted to abandon mental prayer, arguing "I am full of faults, I'm not making any progress, I'm incapable of being really converted and loving God seriously. Presenting myself before him in such a state is just hypocrisy—I'm pretending to be a saint, when I am worth no more than people who don't pray at all. It would be much more honest in God's eyes if I just dropped it completely!"

St. Teresa let herself be fooled by this argument. As she tells it in chapter 19 of her autobiography, after practicing mental prayer assiduously for some time, she abandoned it for over a year. Then she spoke to a Dominican friar who, luckily for us, put her back on the right path. At the time she was living in the Convent of the Incarnation at Avila. She had sufficient good will to want to give herself to God and practice mental prayer, but she was not yet a saint—far from it! In particular, although she knew Jesus was asking her to stop, she could not break the habit of going to the convent parlor where—happy, friendly, and affectionate by nature—she took great pleasure in conversing with Avila's high society. She was not doing anything really wrong, but Jesus was calling her to something else. Mental prayer became a real torture to her; she found herself in the presence of our Lord, aware of being unfaithful to him, but without the strength to give up everything for him. She thought: "I am unworthy to come before the Lord, since I am not capable of giving him everything. I'm not taking him seriously—it would be better to stop praying. . . ."

St. Teresa of Avila later called this a temptation to "false humility." She had in fact abandoned mental prayer when a confessor made her realize just in time that in so doing she was also abandoning every chance of ever improving. She had to do just the opposite: persevere, because it was precisely by perseverance that she would obtain, in due course, the grace of a complete conversion and of giving herself totally to our Lord.

This is very important. When we start doing mental prayer we are not saints, and the more we do it the more we realize that fact. People who never come face to face with God in silence are never really conscious of their infidelities and faults, but when we pray, such things become much more obvious. That may give rise to a lot of suffering and the temptation to stop praying. We should not be discouraged at that stage, but should persevere, convinced that perseverance will obtain for us the grace of conversion. Our sinfulness, however grave, should *never* be an excuse to abandon prayer, contrary to what we may imagine or the devil may suggest. Just the opposite: the more wretched we are, the more motivated we should be to do mental prayer. Who will heal us of our infidelities and sins if not our merciful Lord? Where will we find health for our souls except in humble, persevering prayer? "It is not those who are healthy who need a doctor, but those who are sick. I have not come to call the just, but sinners" (Mt 9: 13). The illness which is sin should spur us on to do mental prayer. Wounded as we are, we must take refuge in the Heart of Jesus! He alone can cure us. If we wait until we are just or righteous before doing mental prayer, we may have to wait a very long time. Thinking like that would only prove we had not understood a word of the Gospel. It might look like humility, but it would only be presumption and lack of trust in God.

Not infrequently it happens that, having committed some fault and feeling ashamed and unhappy, without entirely giving up on prayer we let a little time pass—until the echo of the sin has stopped reverberating in conscience—before resuming it and once more entering into the Lord's presence. That is a very serious mistake, more sinful than the original fault. It shows a lack of trust in God's mercy and ignorance of his love, and those slights wound him far more than whatever stupid things we may have done. St. Thérèse of Lisieux, who understood who God is, said, "What hurts God, what wounds his heart, is a lack of trust." When we have sinned, the just reaction— "just" in the biblical sense, meaning in conformity with what has been revealed to us about the mystery of God—is exactly the opposite. It is to throw ourselves at once, with repentance and humility—and also with unlimited trust—into the arms of God's mercy, certain that we will be welcomed and forgiven. Having sincerely told God we're sorry, we should take up our usual prayers again without delay, especially our mental prayer. Confession is necessary, we will confess our fault as soon as we can, but we will not change any of our habits of prayer in the meantime. This is the surest way of being freed from sin because it is the way that most honors God's mercy.

St. Teresa of Avila adds something very beautiful in this regard. She says that people who do mental prayer of course continue to fall, to have failures and faults, but because they pray, each fall helps them to spring back even higher. God makes all things—even their falls—work together for the good and the progress of those who are faithful to mental prayer.

> I stress this, so that none of those who have begun to do mental prayer should stop again with the excuse that "If I am falling back into sin and still continue to pray, it will be even worse." I think it would be worse if they abandoned their mental prayer and did not correct the sin; but if they do not abandon mental prayer, let them believe that this prayer will lead them to the harbor of light. The devil waged such a combat against me with that purpose, and I believed for so long that to do mental prayer was a lack of humility when I was so wicked, that, as I said, I stopped

doing it for a year and a half, (or a year at any rate, I'm not quite sure about the half). And that would have been enough, and was enough, for me to throw my own self into hell with no need for any devil to drag me down there. O God, what blindness! And how right the devil was, in aiming for his goal, to concentrate his forces on this point! He knows, the traitor, that whoever perseveres in mental prayer is lost to him, that all the falls he may cause them only help them, through God's goodness, to spring back even higher in God's service; so it matters to him a lot.[4]

8. *Total self-giving to God*

There is a close, two-way connection between mental prayer and the rest of one's Christian life. The result is that very often what determines our progress and deepening in mental prayer is not what we do during prayer time but the rest of the time. Progress in prayer is essentially progress in love, in purity of heart; and true love is put into practice more outside prayer than in it. Let's look at some examples.

We are deluding ourselves in aiming to make progress in mental prayer if our whole life is not marked by a deep, sincere desire to give ourselves totally to God, to make our lives conform to his will as fully as possible. Without that desire, prayer life stalls and progresses no further. God only gives himself to us (which is the goal of mental prayer) if we give ourselves totally to him. We can only

[4] *Autobiography*, chap. 19.

possess everything by giving everything. If we keep a sealed-off compartment in our lives that we don't want to abandon to God—a fault, for example, even a very little one, which we consent to deliberately and do nothing to correct; or a conscious piece of disobedience, or a refusal to forgive someone—it will make our life of prayer unfruitful.

Some nuns once asked St. John of the Cross, "What must one do in order to enter into ecstasy?" And the saint answered by considering the etymological meaning of the word. "One must renounce one's own will and do the will of God. For ecstasy is nothing other for the soul than coming out of itself and being swept away into God—and that is what the person who obeys does, for he comes out of himself and his own will, and lightened of all that, he attaches himself to God." [5]

To give oneself to God one must leave one's own self behind. Love is ecstatic by nature: in loving strongly, one lives in the other more than in oneself. But how could we practice that ecstatic dimension of love in our prayer, even to a small degree, if for the rest of the day we seek ourselves? If we are too attached to material things, our comfort, and our vanity? If we cannot bear the slightest setback? How can we live in God if we cannot forget ourselves for the sake of our brothers and sisters?

There is a balance to be sought in the spiritual life, and finding it is not always easy. On the one hand we must

[5] Maxim 210.

accept the fact of our wretchedness and not put off doing mental prayer until we become saints. On the other hand, we must aspire to be perfect. Without that strong, constant desire for holiness—even if we know very well that we will not attain it by our own strength and God alone can bring us to holiness!—mental prayer will never be anything other than superficial, a pious exercise but nothing more, and it will produce very little fruit. It is love's nature to tend toward the absolute—toward a giving of self that has about it a kind of madness.

We should also be aware that our whole lifestyle can favor or hinder mental prayer. How can we be recollected in God's presence if all the rest of the time we are distracted by a thousand superficial concerns and worries, if we take part in pointless gossip, if we fail to discipline our hearts and eyes and minds, so as to refrain from everything that could turn us away from what is Essential?

Of course no one can live without some amusement and times of relaxation. What matters is that we be always able to return to God[6] (since it is he who supplies the unity of our lives) and to live every moment under his eyes and in contact with him.

Something else also contributes greatly to the growth of our prayer life—namely, the effort to face every circumstance with an attitude of total abandonment and

---

[6] In fact, some spiritual authors go further and say that, for the ordinary Christian seeking holiness, God is to be found precisely in all noble human activities, including leisure and entertainment.

peaceful trust in God, to live in the present moment without fretting about tomorrow's cares, to do everything we do peacefully, without worrying about what comes next. It isn't easy, but if we put our hearts into it, the effort will bear fruit.

It is also very important little by little to learn to live out every part of our lives under God's eyes, in his presence and in a sort of ongoing dialogue with him, recalling him as often as possible in the middle of our occupations and keeping him company in all we do. The more we try to do this, the easier mental prayer will become. (It's easier to find God in times of prayer if we have never left him!) Thus the practice of mental prayer should lead to continual prayer, not necessarily explicit, verbal prayer, but rather a constant awareness of God's presence. Living under God's gaze like that will set us free. Too often, when we feel other people's eyes on us, it is because we fear their judgment or crave their admiration; and if we are always watching ourselves, that may be complacency at work—or guilt. But in learning to live under God's merciful, loving gaze, we find only inner freedom.

Some advice by Brother Lawrence of the Resurrection can be very valuable for developing "the practice of the presence of God." This seventeenth-century Carmelite friar, a cook, learned to live in profound union with God amidst the most absorbing activities. Some extracts from his writings will be found at the end of this book.

There is much more to say about the link between

mental prayer and the rest of the spiritual life. Some points will be covered later. For the rest, the best suggestion is to consult the best possible source—that is, the experience of the saints, especially those in whom the Church has recognized a special gift for teaching others in this area: St. Teresa of Avila, St. John of the Cross, St. Francis de Sales, and St. Thérèse of Lisieux, to name a few.

But how should one do mental prayer? Specifically, how should one spend the time allotted to it? This question will be considered shortly. But the preliminaries we've been discussing were absolutely indispensable and should help overcome some obstacles. Once someone grasps the spiritual attitudes sketched here, many false problems about how to pray will simply disappear.

These attitudes are not based on human wisdom but on the Gospel. They are attitudes of faith, trusting abandonment in God's hands, humility, poverty of heart, and spiritual childhood. They should form the basis not just of our prayer life but the whole of our existence. Here again we see the close link between prayer and life as a whole: prayer is a school, an exercise in which we understand, practice, and deepen certain attitudes toward God, ourselves, and other people—attitudes that gradually become fundamental to our whole way of being and acting. Through mental prayer, we stamp our lives with a certain pattern, present in all we do, that enables us, little by little, to achieve peace, inner freedom, and true love for God and neighbor in all circumstances. Mental prayer is a school of love, because the virtues practiced in prayer are ones that enable love to take hold in our heart. This is why mental prayer is of such vital importance.

II How to use the time of mental prayer

1. *Introductory ideas*

"I have decided to spend half an hour or an hour every day doing mental prayer. How should I set about it? What should I do to use this time well?" This is not an easy question to answer, for three reasons.

First, souls are very different. There are more differences between people's souls than between people's faces. Each person's relationship with God is unique, and therefore each person's prayer is unique. No one can map out a path or method that applies to everyone, because that would mean disregarding people's freedom and the diversity of their spiritual journeys. It is up to each believer to discover, in response to the Spirit's movement and in the freedom of the Spirit, the path along which God wishes to lead him or her.

Second, the life of prayer is subject to development and goes through stages. What applies at a certain point in our spiritual life does not apply at another point. The right way of proceeding in mental prayer can be very different depending on whether someone is at the beginning of the way or our Lord has already begun to introduce that individual to certain specific states, that St. Teresa of Avila would call "dwellings." Sometimes we have to act; sometimes we must be content to receive. Sometimes we have to rest; sometimes we have to fight.

Third, what is experienced in mental prayer is difficult to describe. Often the person experiencing it has no clear consciousness of it. We are in the presence here of inner, mysterious realities that cannot be fully expressed in human language. Words are often lacking to express what happens between the soul and its God. Moreover, everyone who speaks about the life of prayer does so in reference to their own experience, or what others have confided to them. It is very little compared with the diversity and richness of the totality of prayer experiences.

Despite these obstacles, I am going to tackle the subject now, hoping the Lord will give me the grace to set out a few indications that, though not the total and infallible answer to particular cases, may nevertheless offer light and encouragement for readers of good will.

2. *When the question does not arise*

So, how should we spend the time of mental prayer? Let's start by recognizing that sometimes the question does not come up.

That is so when mental prayer flows naturally, so to speak; when there is a loving communion between ourselves and God, with no need to ask how to spend the time. Indeed, it should always be like that, since prayer, according to St. Teresa of Avila, is "an intimate commerce of friendship where one often goes to speak alone with God, by whom one knows oneself to be loved" (*Autobiography*, chap. 8). Two people who love each other deeply don't usually have many problems about how to spend their time together. Sometimes just being together is enough—they don't need to do anything else! But often, alas, our love for God is very weak, and we don't reach that level.

This sort of prayer that "flows naturally," this communion with God that comes by itself and we need only accept, may occur at different stages of the spiritual journey and may be of very different kinds.

Often, for instance, that is how it is with recent converts, overflowing with enthusiasm for their newly discovered God and full of the joy and fervor of the newborn. They have no problem with prayer. Borne along by grace, delighted to dedicate time to Jesus, they have a thousand things to tell him and ask him, and they are full of feelings of love and strengthening thoughts.

They should have no scruple about enjoying that time of grace, and should thank our Lord for it. But they also should stay humble, and beware of believing they are holy because of their fervor, or judge their neighbor less zealous than themselves. The grace of those first moments of conversion has not removed their faults and imperfections, only covered them over. They should not be surprised if one fine day fervor vanishes, and faults that they thought their conversion had freed them from return with unexpected force. Now is the time for them to persevere and learn to draw as much profit from the arid desert of their trials as they did from the time of God's blessings.

Often, too, the question of how to spend time in prayer does not come up at the other end of the journey. Then God may take possession of people in their prayer to such an extent that they cannot resist or do anything for themselves: their faculties are taken captive, and all they can do is let go and consent to the presence of God who invades their whole being. There is nothing for them to do but say yes. Nevertheless, such people should open their souls to a spiritual director in order to receive confirmation that the graces they are receiving are genuine, since at this stage they are no longer on well-trodden paths and need to open up honestly to someone else. Extraordinary graces in prayer often are succeeded by conflicts and doubts when they cease and uncertainty as to their cause. Sometimes only opening one's heart to a spiritual director can bring reassurance concerning their divine origin and set a person free to respond to them fully.

There also is an intermediate case, quite common, and worth speaking of because the situation sometimes begins almost imperceptibly, and people may feel doubts or scruples about how to react: not sure if they are doing right or wrong, but apparently having no choice in the matter in either case. What is happening, in fact, is that the Holy Spirit is beginning to lead the person into a more passive way of mental prayer. Previously his or her prayer has been fairly "active," in the sense that it consisted mainly of reflections, meditation, inner conversation with Jesus, acts of the will such as offering themselves to him.[1] But then, sometimes beginning without their realizing it, their way of praying is transformed. It is difficult to meditate and reason. They have a sort of dryness and feel inclined to stay before our Lord without doing or saying anything, or even thinking anything special, in a peaceful attitude of attention and love toward God. Moreover, that loving attention, proceeding from the heart rather than the mind, is nearly imperceptible. It may become stronger later, transformed into a flame of love, but usually at the start it can hardly be noticed.

If people in this state try to do something else, like going back to a more "active" way of praying, they don't succeed. Instead they almost always tend to revert to the state just described. But they may sometimes worry or have scruples about it, because they have the impression that they are doing nothing now, whereas up till then they had a sense of doing something in mental prayer.

When people find themselves in this state, they should simply remain in it, not worrying or getting agitated. God wants to introduce them to a deeper kind of prayer, and this is a very great grace. They should let him act, and follow their inclination to stay passive. That peaceful ori-

[1] This topic will be dealt with more fully later on, in discussing the development of the life of prayer.

entation toward God in their heart is sufficient for prayer. This is not the time to act on their own account, using their faculties and abilities; it is time to let God act. God is not yet taking total possession of the soul. One's mind and will continue to act to a certain extent: thoughts and images come and go, but these are at surface level, scarcely noticed and more or less involuntary. What matters is not that movement of the mind,[2] but the deep orientation of the heart toward God.

These, then, are a few situations where there is no need to ask "How should I spend my time of mental prayer?" The answer is already given.

Sometimes, though, the question does arise. Generally speaking, this is the case with people who are full of good will, but who are not (not yet!) on fire with love for God and have not yet received the grace of passive prayer. Still, having grasped the importance of mental prayer, they want to dedicate time to it regularly, without really knowing how to go about it. What do you tell them?

I am not going to give a direct answer to the question by saying "During the time of mental prayer you should do this and this, pray like that or that." It seems more advisable to begin by giving the principles that should guide these people in praying.

The preceding chapter explained the basic attitudes. They are valid for all types of prayer and even for the whole of a Christian's life, as was said. What matters is

[1] Distractions are discussed below.

49

not so much methods and instructions as attitude—the disposition of soul with which people embark on prayer. Having the right attitude or disposition is crucial to perseverance and fruitfulness in prayer.

This time I shall give a certain number of guidelines that, taken together, define not so much an attitude as a sort of inner landscape, with landmarks and paths. Those who wish to pray are free to make their own way through the landscape, depending on just where they are in their spiritual journey and which way the Holy Spirit is leading them. Once believers know a little about these landmarks, they can orientate themselves and determine what they need to do.

The "inner landscape" of a Christian's prayer life is defined and shaped by certain theological truths, as follows.

3. *Primacy of God's action*

The first principle is simple but extremely important. What matters in mental prayer is not so much what we do, as what God does in us.

It is enormously liberating to know this, for sometimes we can do nothing at all in mental prayer. Really, though, it doesn't matter much, because even if we can't do anything, God can. In fact, he is always acting in the depths of our soul, even if we don't realize it. The essential act of prayer, after all, is to put oneself in God's presence and stay there. Now God is not the God of the dead but of the living, and his presence, being the presence of the living God, is active, life-giving, healing, and sanctifying. One can't stand in front of a fire without being warmed, or stay in the sun without being tanned, and in remaining in God's presence and letting him act in the depths of our being, we are doing what really counts.

If our prayer consists of nothing more than that—holding ourselves before God without doing anything or thinking of anything special, without any particular feelings, but with a heartfelt attitude of availability and trusting abandonment—then we could not do any better.

We should not measure the value of our mental prayer by how much we do during the time allotted to it, thinking it good and profitable to say and think many things, and getting upset if we haven't been able to do anything. The prayer may indeed have been very poor, and yet God may have worked wonders secretly in one's soul during that time, doing things whose fruits will only become apparent much later. The cause of the immense riches arising from prayer is not our thoughts or our actions, but the action of God in our hearts. Only in the Kingdom of Heaven will we see many of prayer's fruits.

St. Thérèse of Lisieux knew all this. She had a problem in her mental prayer: she used to fall asleep! It wasn't her fault—she was still very young when she entered Carmel, and she wasn't getting enough sleep for her age. But she wasn't overly upset by this weakness:

I think how little children please their parents just as much when they are asleep as when they are awake; I think how doctors put patients to sleep in order to do operations. And finally, I think how "the Lord sees our weakness, he remembers that we are but dust" (*Autobiography*, manuscript A).

The passive component in our prayer is the most important part. Prayer has less to do with doing something than with delivering ourselves up to God's action. Sometimes we need to prepare for or follow up on his action, but very often we have only to consent to it. That is when the most important things happen. Sometimes it is even necessary to halt one's activity so that God can act freely. As St. John of the Cross explained so well, this is what explains certain times of aridity, when it is impossible to make the mind or imagination work or feel anything or meditate. God puts us into that state, a kind of night, so that he alone acts deeply within us, just as a surgeon anaesthetizes a patient so as to be able to work freely!

We will return to this later. For the moment, what we need to grasp is that if, despite having good will, we are incapable of praying well, or producing any good sentiments or beautiful reflections, that should not make us sad. We should offer our poverty to the action of God. Then we will be making a prayer much more valuable than the kind that would leave us feeling self-satisfied. St. Francis de Sales used to pray, "Lord, I am nothing but a block of wood: set fire to it!"

4. *Primacy of love*

The second principle is also absolutely fundamental: *the primacy of love over everything else.* St. Teresa of Avila says, "In prayer, what counts is not to think a lot but to love a lot."

How liberating that is! Sometimes one can't think, can't meditate, can't feel; but one can always love. Instead of worrying and getting discouraged, those who are tired out, tormented by distractions, and incapable of doing mental prayer, can always offer their poverty to our Lord in peaceful trust. If they do that, they are making a magnificent mental prayer. Love is king, and no matter what the circumstances, love always triumphs in the end. "Love draws profit from everything, good and bad alike," St. Thérèse of Lisieux liked to say, quoting St. John of the Cross. Love draws profit from feelings and from dryness, from profound reflections and from aridity, from virtue and from sin, and much more besides.

This principle is connected to the first, the primacy of God's action over ours. Our main task in praying is to love. But in our relationship with God, loving means first of all *letting ourselves be loved.* This isn't as easy as it might seem. It means we have to believe in love, and often we find it very easy to doubt it. It also means we have to accept the fact that we are poor.

Often we find it easier to love than to let ourselves be loved. Doing something, giving something, gratifies us

and makes us feel useful, but letting ourselves be loved
means consenting not to do anything, to be nothing. Our
first task in mental prayer, instead of offering or doing
anything for God, is to let ourselves be loved by him like
very small children. Let God have the joy of loving us.
That is difficult, because it means having a rock-solid
belief in God's love for us. It also implies accepting the
fact of our own poverty. Here we touch on something
absolutely fundamental: there is no true love for God
which is not built on a recognition of the absolute priority
of God's love for us; there is no true love for God that has
not grasped that, before doing anything at all, we have
first to receive. "In this is love," St. John tells us, "not that
we loved God, but that he loved us first" (1 Jn 4: 10).

In the relationship with God our first act of love, one
that must remain the basis for every act of love for him, is
this: to believe that he loves us, and to let ourselves be
loved in our poverty, just as we are, quite apart from any
merits or virtues we may possess. With this as the ground-
ing of our relationship with God, the relationship is on a
sound footing. Otherwise it is distorted by a certain Phari-
seeism, its center not ultimately occupied by God but by
our own selves, our activity, our virtue, or some such thing.

This is a very demanding attitude, since it requires that
we shift the center of our existence from ourselves to God
and forget about ourselves. But it sets us free. God is not
primarily looking for us to do things. We are "unprofitable
servants" (Lk 17: 10). "God does not need our works, but is

thirsty for our love," said St. Thérèse of Lisieux. He asks us first of all to let ourselves be loved, to believe in his love, and that is always possible. Prayer is basically that: to remain in God's presence and let him love us. The response of love comes readily, either during or outside the time of mental prayer. God himself will produce good in us and will enable us to accomplish "the good works which God has prepared beforehand to be our way of life" (Eph 2: 10).

A further consequence of love's primacy is that our activity in mental prayer should be guided by this principle: we should do whatever favors and strengthens love. This is the only criterion for saying it is right or wrong to do this or that in our prayer. Whatever leads to love is right. But it must be true love, obviously, not a superficial, sentimental love—even though burning sentiments, if granted to us by God, do have their value in expressing love.

Thoughts, considerations, and inner acts that nourish or express love for God, make us grow in gratitude and trust toward him, arouse or stimulate desire to give ourselves wholly to him, to belong to him and serve him faithfully as our only Lord—these are what normally make up the greater part of our activity in mental prayer. Everything that strengthens our love for God is a good subject for prayer.

AIM FOR SIMPLICITY   From all this it follows that in mental prayer we mustn't flit from one thing to another or multiply thoughts and considerations, behavior suggesting an interest in flights of fancy rather than real, practical conversion of heart. It would do me little good to entertain lofty thoughts about the mysteries of the faith, then change the focus of my meditation to range through the truths of theology and the whole of Scripture, if in the end I was not more firmly resolved to give myself to God and deny myself for love of him. St. Thérèse of Lisieux says, "To love is to give everything and to give oneself." Mental prayer that every day consists of only one thought, untiringly revisited—to stir up my heart to give itself wholly to our Lord and ceaselessly strengthen my resolution to serve him and surrender myself to his power—then my prayer will have been less grand, but far better.

A telling incident in the life of St. Thérèse of Lisieux sheds light on the primacy of love. Shortly before she died, when she was gravely ill and confined to bed, her sister, Mother Agnes, came into the room and asked, "What are you thinking about?" "I'm not thinking about anything, I'm in too much pain. So I pray." Mother Agnes persisted. "And what do you say to Jesus?" Thérèse said, "I don't say anything. I just love him!"

This is the poorest and deepest kind of prayer: a simple act of love, beyond words and thoughts. We should aspire to the same simplicity. In the end, our mental prayer should be one single, simple act of love. But to reach that simplicity, it takes much time and the operation of grace at a deep level. Sin has made us so complicated and so thoroughly dissipated our faculties.

Remember: the value of mental prayer is not measured by how many things we do. On the contrary: the closer prayer comes to that simple act of love, the more it is worth. Normally, too, prayer becomes more simple the further we progress in the spiritual life. We shall see more about this later.

Before leaving this subject, it is necessary to speak of a temptation that may arise in mental prayer. Sometimes when praying we may think of something very deep and attractive—a new light on the mystery of God or an insight concerning our own life or something like that. Brilliant as they may seem at the time, there often is a danger in such thoughts, and we need to be on our guard. Certainly, God sometimes sends lights and profound inspirations during mental prayer. But in dwelling on these thoughts we may be turning away from a less showy but more authentic presence of God. Enticed, fired with enthusiasm, we may end up paying more attention to our thoughts than to God. When the time of prayer ends, our mental edifice collapses, leaving very little behind.

5. *God gives himself through the humanity of Jesus*

After the primacy of God's action, and the primacy of love, there is a third principle that underpins a Christian's contemplative life: *we find God in the humanity of Jesus*.

The reason we do mental prayer is to enter into communion with God. But no one knows God. So what means do we have for finding him? Jesus Christ, true God and true man, is the only mediator. His humanity, the humanity of God the Son, is the medium of our seeking, finding, and being united to God. As St. Paul says, "In him the whole fullness of Deity dwells bodily" (Col 2:9). The humanity of Jesus is the primordial sacrament through which the Divinity makes itself accessible to human beings.

As creatures of flesh and blood, we need the support of material things in order to attain to spiritual realities. God knows this, and it is what explains the whole mystery of the Incarnation. We need to see, to touch, to feel. Jesus Christ's visible, physical humanity is the expression of God's wonderful condescension toward us. Knowing what we are made of, he gives us the possibility of reaching divine things in a human way, touching what is divine by human means. Spirit has become flesh. Jesus is the way to God for us. St. Philip asked Jesus, "Lord, show us the Father, and we will be satisfied," and Jesus answered, "Whoever has seen me has seen the Father" (Jn 14:8-9).

There is a great and very beautiful mystery here. The humanity of Jesus in all its aspects, even those that are apparently humblest and least important, is for us an immense *space for communion with God*. Every aspect of his humanity, each of his characteristics, even the smallest and most hidden, each of his words, deeds, and gestures, every stage of his life from his conception in Mary's womb to his Ascension, brings us into communion with God the Father if we receive it in faith. By exploring his humanity like a piece of land that belongs to us, going through it like a book written especially for us, making it our own in faith and love, we grow steadily in communion with the inaccessible, unfathomable mystery of God.

A Christian's mental prayer will, then, always be based on a certain relationship with our Savior's humanity.[3] The different forms of Christian mental prayer, of which we shall give some examples shortly, are alike in finding their theological justification in the fact that they bring us into communion with God by means of the humanity of Jesus. Since Jesus Christ's humanity is a kind of sacrament—an efficacious sign of man's union with God—it is enough for us to be linked in faith with that humanity in order to enter into communion with God.

Bérulle[4] beautifully expresses the extent to which the mysteries of Jesus' life, though in the past, remain living and life-giving realities for those who contemplate them in faith.

> We must posit the perpetual nature of these mysteries in some way, for they are past in certain circumstances, and they are lasting and are present and perpetual in a certain other way. They are past as regards their execution, but they are present as regards their virtue, and their virtue

[3] As is well known, St. Teresa of Avila was strongly attached to this truth, in opposition to certain people who taught that to reach union with God and pure contemplation it was necessary to reach the point of abandoning all reference to everything connected with the senses, even our Lord's humanity. See her *Autobiography*, chap. 22, and *Sixth Dwellings*, VII.

[4] Cardinal Pierre de Bérulle (1575–1629) founded the French Oratorians and wrote several works on theology and spirituality.

never passes away; nor does the love with which they were accomplished ever pass away. So that the spirit, the state, the virtue, the merit of the mystery is always present. . . . That obliges us to treat the things and mysteries pertaining to Jesus not as things which are past and dead, but as things living and present, from which we too have to harvest fruits which are present and eternal.

For example, he applies this to Jesus' childhood:

The childhood of the Son of God is a transitory state: the circumstances of that childhood are past, and he is no longer a child. But there is something divine in this mystery which continues in existence in heaven and which brings about a similar manner of grace in the souls of those people on earth whom it pleases Jesus Christ to attach and dedicate to that first humble state of his human life.

There are a multitude of ways of being in contact with the humanity of Jesus. We can contemplate his deeds and gestures, meditate on his actions and words, on the events of his life on earth, and keep them in memory, we can look at his face in an icon, adore him in his Body in the Eucharist, pronounce his Name lovingly and keep it in our heart, and so on. All these things sustain us in mental prayer, provided only that we do not do them out of intellectual curiosity but in a loving search for Jesus: "I sought him whom my soul loves" (Song 3: 1).

Intellectual speculation is not what enables us to gaze upon Jesus' humanity in such a way that we enter through it into real communion with the unfathomable mystery of God. This comes about through faith—faith as a theological virtue, faith enlivened by love. This faith alone (St. John of the Cross laid special stress on the point) empowers us to enter into the mystery of God through the person of Christ. This is the faith by which we cling with all our being to Christ, in whom God gives himself to us.

And that is why for a Christian the privileged way of doing mental prayer is by communing with the humanity of Jesus, by whatever means or methods.

So, for instance, one classic method, at least in the West, is that recommended by St. Teresa of Avila: to live in Jesus' company, as one would live with a friend with whom one converses.

> We can picture ourselves standing in front of Christ, and arouse in ourselves the liveliest sentiments of love for his Sacred Humanity; live in his presence, talk to him, ask him for the things we need, tell him about the things that are making us suffer, share our joys with him instead of letting them drive him from our thoughts; without looking for well-turned phrases in our prayers, but finding the words that express our desires and needs. This is an excellent way of making very rapid progress; those who make this effort to live in his precious company so as to profit greatly from it and experience real love for our Lord, to whom we owe so much—those are souls I consider to be very advanced (*Autobiography*, chap. 12).

We shall come back to this point.

6. *God dwells in our hearts*

Our fourth theological principle also offers powerful guidance in the life of prayer. By mental prayer we are trying to join ourselves to God's presence. But as the modes of that presence are multiple, so are there many different ways of praying. God is present in his creation, and we can contemplate him there; he is present in the Eucharist, and we can adore him there; he is present in the Word, and we can find God by meditating on Scripture. And so on.

There is, however, another mode of God's presence of the greatest importance for the life of prayer: *God's presence in our own heart.*

As with the other forms of the presence of God, this presence within ourselves is not something experienced (though we may approach that, little by little, at least at certain privileged moments) but something known by faith. Regardless of what we may or may not feel, we are certain through faith that God dwells in the depths of our hearts. "Do you not know that your body is a temple of the Holy Spirit within you?" says St. Paul (1 Cor 6: 19). St. Teresa of Avila herself tells how this truth, once grasped, profoundly transformed her prayer life.

> It is clear to me that if I had understood, as I do today, that in this tiny palace of my soul, such a great King is living, I would not have left him alone so often, I would have gone to seek him out from time to time, and I would have taken steps to ensure that the palace was less dirty. How

admirable it is, then, to think that he whose greatness would fill a thousand worlds and much more, shuts himself into such a little thing! In truth, since he is the Master, he is free, and since he loves us, he reduces himself to the measure of our smallness.[5]

Here is the truth that confers meaning upon the element of recollection and inwardness in mental prayer. Otherwise recollection would be mere self-absorption. Christians can legitimately enter into themselves because, beyond and deeper than all their inner wretchedness, they find God, "more intimate to us than we ourselves," as St. Augustine put it; God who dwells in us through the grace of the Holy Spirit. "The deepest center of the soul," says St. John of the Cross, "is God."[6]

Entering into his own heart in faith, man unites himself there to this presence. Sometimes in mental prayer we unite ourselves to God as Other, external to ourselves, and present in a pre-eminent way in the humanity of Jesus. But sometimes in prayer we enter into the interior of our own heart and there meet Jesus, so close and so accessible to us.

> "Who will go up to heaven and get it for us. . . . Who will cross to the other side of the sea for us? . . . No, the word is very near to you; it is in your mouth and in your heart" (Deut 30: 12-14).

[5] *Way of Perfection*, chap. 28.
[6] *Living Flame of Love*, strophe 1, line 3.

Do you think it is nothing to an anguished soul to grasp this truth, to see that she does not need to go up to heaven to speak to her eternal Father and enjoy his company, and that she does not have to shout to make herself heard by him? However softly we speak, he is so close to us that he can hear us; nor do we need wings to go in search of him, but merely to seek solitude and contemplate him within ourselves, without being surprised to find such a good Guest there. In all humility, let us speak to him as to a father, tell him our needs as we would tell our father, tell him about our sufferings and ask him to remedy them, while fully realizing that we are not worthy to be his children.[7]

When we don't know how to pray, the simplest thing to do is recollect ourselves, keep silence, and enter into our own heart, go down into ourselves and, by faith, rejoin the presence of Jesus who dwells within us, and stay peacefully with him. Don't leave him alone, keep him company. Someone who perseveres in doing this will soon discover the reality of what Eastern Christians call the "place of the heart"—the "inner cell," as St. Catherine of Siena called it. This is the center of our being, where God has taken up his abode and we can always be with him. Yet many men and women do not know about this inner space of communion with God because they have never gone there, never visited this garden to gather its fruits. Happy are they who make the discovery of *the Kingdom of God within themselves*. It will change their lives.

[7] Ibid.

True, the human heart is an abyss of wretchedness and sin, but deeper still than all that, there is God. St. Teresa of Avila said a person who perseveres in mental prayer is like someone going to get water from a well—he lets down the bucket and at first all he draws up is mud; but if he has trust and perseveres the day will come when he finds the purest water. "Let anyone who is thirsty come to me, and let the one who believes in me drink. As Scripture has said, 'Out of the believer's heart shall flow rivers of living water'" (Jn 7: 38).

This is a truth of immense importance for the whole of life. If by persevering in mental prayer we discover that "place of the heart," little by little our thoughts, choices, and actions, which all too often spring from superficial levels (our worries, annoyances, immediate reactions), will begin to have their source in the deep center of the soul where we are united to God in love. Then everything will proceed from love, and then we will be free.

*

These, then, are the four great principles that should guide us in mental prayer: the primacy of God's action, the primacy of love, the humanity of Jesus as an instrument of communion with God, and God's dwelling within our heart. These principles are points of reference that help us pray well.

But we also need to be aware of the development of the prayer life, the stages of the spiritual life. That is the next subject.

III   The development of the life of prayer

1. *From the mind to the heart*

The life of prayer is not static. It develops in stages and makes progress—progress that is not always in a straight line but sometimes even seems to fall back.

Spiritual writers usually distinguish "states of prayer," from the most ordinary up to the most sublime, that the journey of the soul makes in reaching union with God. The number of these phases and their names vary from author to author. St. Teresa of Avila speaks of seven dwellings; other writers distinguish three stages (purgative, illuminative, unitive); certain authors say meditation is followed by affective prayer, then the prayer of simple contemplation, then the prayer of quietude, after which they speak of the sleep of the faculties, rapture, ecstasy, and so on.

It is not my intention to go into detail about stages in the life of prayer and mystical graces and trials encountered on the way, though these are more common than many people think. The readers for whom this book is meant have no immediate need for all that. (And highly schematic accounts of stages in the interior life should probably not be taken too literally anyway, especially in a time and place when God in his wisdom often seems to operate by a different set of rules.)

That said, however, it is necessary to speak of what I consider the first great change, the fundamental transformation of the life of prayer. All subsequent developments are only consequences of this first one.

This transformation may be given different names by different spiritual traditions or writers, but it seems to me that it is to be found more or less everywhere, even when the spiritual paths being recommended or described have widely differing starting points. In the West, for example, which habitually proposes meditation as the starting point for mental prayer (or rather used to propose it, since people today often come to the life of prayer by different routes) it is spoken of as the passage from *meditation* to *contemplation*. St. John of the Cross has written about it at length, giving a full description of this stage and the criteria for identifying it.

The Eastern tradition of the Jesus Prayer [1] (also called the Prayer of the Heart), popularized in the West in the twentieth century by the book *The Way of the Pilgrim*, takes as its starting point the tireless repetition of the name of Jesus. It speaks of this transforming stage as a time when prayer passes "from the mind into the heart."

Basically, these are different ways of describing the same phenomenon, even though this transformation, which can also be described as a simplification that shifts from an

[1] This prayer is described in more detail later.

"active" to a more "passive" kind of prayer, may have very different manifestations depending on the individual.

What does the transformation consist of? It is a special gift from God, received suddenly by people who have persevered in prayer. It cannot be acquired by force, but is a pure grace—although faithfulness to mental prayer plays a large part in preparing for it and making it more likely. It may come very soon, sometimes only after years, sometimes not at all. It is often almost unnoticed at first. It can be transient, especially at the beginning, and come and go.

The essential characteristic of this gift is that it moves the person praying on to a stage different from the one in which human activity predominates. (The "human activity" may have been the voluntary repetition of a form of words, as in the Jesus Prayer, or reasoning, as in the case of meditation, which involves choosing a text or subject and considering it, working on it with one's thoughts and imagination, and drawing out affections and resolutions.) The new stage is a kind of prayer in which God's action gradually predominates, while the soul lets itself be acted upon rather than acting, keeping itself in an attitude of simplicity, abandonment, and loving, peaceful attention toward God.

In the case of the Jesus Prayer, one experiences the prayer flowing spontaneously in one's heart and filling it with peace, contentment, and love. In the case of meditation, entry into the new stage is often marked by a sort of dryness, an inability to make one's thought processes work, and a tendency to remain in God's presence without doing anything—not out of inertia or spiritual laziness but in a loving abandonment of self.

This transformation should be received as a major grace, even though somewhat disconcerting for people previously accustomed to say a lot to our Lord or to meditate successfully. Now they have the impression that they are going backwards, that their prayer is becoming poorer, that they are powerless to pray. They can no longer pray as they used to, with their mind and reason, using thoughts, images, and things they took pleasure in.

St. John of the Cross had to work hard (and even argue quite bluntly against certain spiritual directors who did not understand this reality at all)[2] to convince people given this grace that they should welcome it. This impoverishment was their true enrichment, he said, and they should not try to return to their former habit of meditation. They should be content to stay before God in an attitude of self-forgetfulness and simple, loving, peaceful attentiveness.

Why is this impoverishment something enriching?

St. John of the Cross explained clearly the simple, fundamental reason why the shift to this new stage is a very important grace. Everything we can understand or even imagine or feel about God is not yet God. God is infinitely beyond every image, every representation,

[2] See especially *The Living Flame of Love*, strophe 3, line 3.

every perception open to our senses. But he is not beyond faith and not beyond love. Faith, said St. John, a master of mystical theology, is the only means capable of uniting us to God. So, the only act that puts us in real contact with God is an act of faith, understood as a simple, loving movement of clinging to God who reveals himself and gives himself in Jesus.

To approach God in prayer by reasoning, reflection, imagination, and enjoyment can be good. As long as that approach does us good and draws us to conversion, strengthens our faith and love, we should use it. But we cannot attain God in his essence by these means, since he is beyond the reach of our intelligence and feelings. Only faith enlivened by love gives access to God himself. And that faith can only be fully exercised by a sort of detachment from sense-images and enjoyment. That is why God sometimes seemingly withdraws from us so only faith can still operate.

When we no longer think, no longer rely on images, feel nothing in particular, but simply remain in an attitude of loving adherence to God, we may have the impression that we are doing nothing and that nothing is happening. But it is then that God communicates himself to us secretly in a much deeper and more substantial way.

Prayer now becomes a deep outpouring of love, sometimes perceptible and sometimes not, in which God and the soul give themselves to one another. This is contemplation, according to St. John of the Cross: the "secret, peaceful, loving infusion" by which God gives himself to us. God pours himself into the soul and the soul pours itself into God by the working of the Holy Spirit in our soul.

Words cannot do justice to what then is happening; but it is something many people experience in prayer, often without being conscious of it. Just as Monsieur Jourdain (in Molière's play *Le Bourgeois Gentilhomme*) was "speaking in prose" without knowing it, many are contemplatives without realizing the depth of their prayer. And it is much better that they don't.

Whatever the starting point of their life of prayer—and as has been said, different people may have very different starting points— it is to this end, or at least this stage, that our Lord wishes to bring very many of them. (After that there is no end to the further stages, the still higher graces, to which the Holy Spirit may lead them, but we shall not go into these here.)

For example, prayer traditions such as the Jesus Prayer and that represented by St. John of the Cross are entirely different and propose widely divergent routes. However, when it comes to describing the grace of contemplation to which both lead, they use strikingly similar language. When St. John of the Cross describes contemplation as "a sweet respiration of love" (in *The Living Flame of Love*), it sounds like something straight out of the *Philokalia*.[3]

[3] Well known in the Near East and Eastern Europe, especially Russia, this is a classic work which collects from the Eastern Fathers and Orthodox spiritual writers texts related to the Jesus Prayer.

2. *The wound in the heart*

It is time to sum up what has been said up to this point and tie together various strands or themes: the primacy of love, contemplation, the prayer of the heart, the humanity of Jesus, and so on.

Experience shows that to pray well and to be brought to the state of passive prayer in which God and the soul communicate in depth, *the heart must be pierced*—pierced, that is, by the love of God, wounded by thirst for the Beloved. Only through such a wound can prayer truly descend into the heart and lodge there. God must touch us at such a deep level of our being that we cannot do without him any more. Without that wound of love, mental prayer will ultimately be no more than a mental exercise or pious spiritual practice; it will never be intimate communion with the one whose own Heart was pierced with love for us.

We have seen that Jesus' humanity mediates between God and mankind. At the center of his humanity is his wounded Heart. It was torn open so that God's love could be poured out on us and we could have access to God. Only when our own hearts too have been laid open by a wound will we be able to receive that outpouring of love. Then a true exchange of love, the goal of the life of prayer, can occur. Then our prayer can become what it is meant to be: a heart-to-Heart.

This wound produced in us by love may take many

different forms at different times: desire, an eager search for the Beloved; repentance and sorrow for sins; thirst for God; agony at his absence. It may be a sweetness that swells the soul; it may be an inexpressible joy; it may be a burning, passionate flame. It will make us into beings forevermore marked by God, with no other life than the life of God within us.

When God our Lord reveals himself to us, he is seeking, naturally, to heal us from bitterness, faults, true or false guilt, hardness, and much more. We know this, and we yearn for his acts of healing. But it is important to understand that in a certain sense he seeks to wound us even more than to heal us. It is by wounding us more and more deeply that he will bring about our true cure. Whether he comes close to us or seems far off, whether he is tender or seems indifferent (and there is all of this in a person's prayer life!) what he does is done always with the aim of wounding us more deeply with his love.

St. Francis de Sales, in his *Treatise on the Love of God*, has a beautiful chapter showing God's different methods of wounding souls with love. For example:

> This poor soul, which is resolved to die rather than offend its God, and yet does not feel a single flicker of fervor but just the reverse, an extreme coldness that leaves it numb, and so weak that it constantly falls into really obvious imperfections, —this soul is deeply wounded, because its love suffers greatly on seeing that God pretends not to see how much it loves him, leaving it as if it were something

that did not belong to him; and it seems to the soul that amidst all its faults, distractions and coldness, our Lord lets fly at it with this reproach: "How can you say that you love me, since your soul is not with me?" This is like a dart of pain through its heart, but the pain comes from love, because if the soul did not love, it would not suffer as it does from the fear of not loving (*Treatise on the Love of God*, book 6, chap. 14).

Sometimes God wounds us more effectively by leaving us in our wretchedness than by healing us of it!

In point of fact, God is less concerned to make us perfect than to attach us firmly to him. One sort of perfection (according to the image we often have of it) would make us self-sufficient and independent. Being wounded in this way makes us poorer, but brings us into communion with God. And that is what counts: not attaining ideal perfection, but being unable to do without God, being constantly bound to him, by our wretchedness as much as by our virtues, so that his love can pour itself into us unceasingly and we somehow give ourselves entirely to him because we have no alternative. This attachment will sanctify us and bring us to perfection.

Here is the explanation of many things in the spiritual life. Now we can see why Jesus did not deliver Paul from the "thorn in his flesh," the "angel of Satan sent to buffet him," but only answered his appeal with: "My grace is sufficient for you, because my power is shown forth in weakness" (2 Cor 12: 9).

This also explains why the poor and the little ones, those who have been wounded by life, often have gifts of prayer not found among the well-to-do.

Above all, mental prayer ultimately consists of keeping this wound of love open, preventing it from healing over. Here is yet another guide to what we should do in prayer. When the smarting of the wound becomes less keen through routine, laziness, and loss of our first love, then we need to take action, wake up, stir up the heart and stimulate it to love by making use of good thoughts and resolutions. As St. Teresa of Avila puts it, we need to strain to draw up the water we need, until our Lord takes pity on us and makes it rain.[4] That can require us to persevere. "I will rise now and go about the city, in the streets and in the squares; I will seek him whom my soul loves" (Song 3: 2).

If, however, the heart is open and God's love is being poured out in us, we need simply to surrender ourselves to that outpouring without doing anything except consent to it or else doing what that love itself prompts us to do by way of response. The outpouring of God's love may perhaps come forcefully, but it may also come with great gentleness, for the movements of divine love are sometimes almost imperceptible; in either case, the heart is awake and attentive — "I slept, but my heart was awake" (Song 5: 2).

[4] St. Teresa of Avila develops this image of water in detail in her *Autobiography*, chaps. 11ff.

In these spiritually impoverished times, I believe that God is directing an especially urgent response to us in our state of woundedness. As a result, the traditional stages of progress in the spiritual life are frequently turned upside-down. People are often propelled into mental prayer without passing through preliminary stages, and may receive the "wound" described here almost immediately. It may come with the grace of conversion; or through the experience of the outpouring of the Holy Spirit, which can happen in charismatic renewal and elsewhere; or through a providential time of trial through which God takes hold of us.

Our part in the life of prayer then consists of being faithful to prayer, persevering in intimate dialogue with God who has reached out to us. When that special experience of God becomes less vivid, we must not, little by little, forget what happened and allow it to be buried under the dust of routine, forgetfulness, and doubt.

3. *Our hearts and the Church's heart*

Finally, a few points about the ecclesiastical dimension of the life of prayer. It would be totally false to suppose that the ecclesiastical dimension, which is such an essential part of Christian life, has little or nothing to do with one's prayer. There is an extremely deep, though sometimes unseen, link connecting the life of the Church and her mission with what happens between the soul and God in the intimacy of prayer. With good reason was a Carmelite nun who never left her convent, St. Thérèse of Lisieux, declared the patron saint of missions.

Much could be said about the relationship between mission and contemplation, how contemplation brings us into the heart of the mystery of the Church and the Communion of Saints, and related subjects.

The grace of prayer always integrates the one praying more fully into the mystery of the Church. This is clear in the Carmelite tradition which of all the monastic traditions is in a sense the most contemplative one in its insistence that the goal is union with God through prayer, along a route that from the outside might seem highly individualistic. At the same time, however, it is the Carmelite tradition that makes clearest the close connection and interdependence between the contemplative life and the mystery of the Church. This connection is simple and very deep: it is brought about by love, because all that matters between God and the soul is Love; and in the ecclesiology implicit in the teachings of the great representatives of Carmel (St. Teresa of Avila, St. John of the Cross, St. Thérèse of Lisieux), Love also constitutes the essence of the mystery of the Church. The Love uniting God and the soul and the Love that constitutes the deepest reality of the Church are one and the same—love that is the gift of the Holy Spirit.

As she was dying, St. Teresa of Avila said, "I am a daughter of the Church." Her first reason for founding her Carmels, placing nuns in cloisters and urging them toward the mystical life, was to respond to the needs of the Church in her time. She was deeply shaken by the ravages of the Protestant Reformation and by the tales of the "conquistadors" about the huge numbers of pagans to be won for Christ. "The world is on fire," she said, "and this is no time to be concerned with unimportant things."

St. John of the Cross states very clearly that disinterested love for God, love freely given to God in prayer, is of the greatest benefit to the Church and what she needs most. "One act of pure love profits the Church more than all the good works in the world."

But it was St. Thérèse of Lisieux who most fully and beautifully expressed the link between personal love for God, lived out in prayer, and the mystery of the Church. She entered Carmel, she said, "to pray for priests and for great sinners," and the turning point of her life came when she discovered the fullness of her vocation.

She had wanted to have all vocations, because she wanted to love Jesus to the point of madness and serve the Church in all possible ways. The breadth of her desires tormented her. She found peace of soul only when she realized, with the help of Scripture, that the greatest service she could render the Church, one that contained all others in itself, was to keep ablaze in herself the fire of love. "Without that love, the missionaries will stop announcing the Gospel, the martyrs will cease to give their lives. . . . At last I have discovered my vocation: in the heart of the Church, Mother, I will be love!" And that love is practiced above all through mental prayer:

I feel that the more the fire of love burns up my heart, the more I say "Draw me to yourself," the more will the souls who turn to me (who would be nothing but a poor little bit of scrap metal if I go away from the divine blaze)—the more those souls will run their fastest to the enchanting perfumes of their Beloved; because a soul that is all burning with love cannot remain inactive; necessarily, like St. Mary Magdalene, it will cling to Jesus' feet, it will listen to his sweet, burning words. Seeming to give nothing, that soul will give much more than Martha who was agitated over many things and wanted her sister to imitate her. . . . All the saints have understood this, and perhaps especially those who filled the universe with the light of the Gospel teachings. Was it not in prayer that Saints Paul, Augustine, John of the Cross, Thomas Aquinas, Francis, Dominic, and so many other illustrious Friends of God, found that divine knowledge which enkindled the greatest minds? A wise man said, "Give me a lever and a fulcrum and I will lift the world." What Archimedes could not obtain, because his plea was not addressed to God, and was only on the level of material things, the Saints have obtained in all fullness. The Almighty has given them as their fulcrum, their point of support, HIS OWN SELF and HIMSELF ALONE. For their lever, he has given them prayer which burns in a flame of love. And that is how they have lifted the world; that is how the saints who are still fighting here below lift it, and how the saints in the future will lift it too, until the end of the world.

St. Thérèse's life exhibits a wonderful mystery: all she ever wanted was a heart-to-heart with Jesus; but the more she centered her being on the love of Jesus, the more her heart grew in love for the Church, becoming as great as the Church, beyond any limit of time and space.[5] The more St. Thérèse lived out in her prayer her vocation of spousal love for Jesus, the more deeply she penetrated into the mystery of the Church. Indeed, this is the only real way to understand the Church. Anyone who does not have a spousal relationship with God in prayer will never perceive the deepest truth of the Church's identity. For the Church is the Spouse of Christ.

In mental prayer, God communicates himself to the soul and causes it to know his desire that all be saved. One's heart becomes identified with Jesus' Heart, sharing his love for his Spouse, the Church, and his thirst to give his life for her and all mankind. "Let the same mind be in you, that was in Christ Jesus," St. Paul exhorts (Phil 2: 5). Without prayer, this identification with Christ cannot be realized.

The charism characteristic of the Carmelite spirit is to show everyone the deep connection between the heart-to-heart intimacy with Jesus found in personal prayer and integration into the heart of the Church. Without question this grace was given to the Carmelites through Mary;

---

[5] See the chapters on St. Thérèse of Lisieux in the beautiful book, by Fr. F. M. Léthel, *Connaître l'amour du Christ qui surpasse toute connaissance* (Editions du Carmel: Toulouse, 1989).

for was not Carmel the first Marian order in the West? And who but Mary, Spouse of the Holy Spirit and type of the Church, could teach this deep wisdom?

IV Material conditions for mental prayer

Next we consider the externals of mental prayer: how long, when, in what physical attitudes, where.

It would be a mistake to attach too much importance to these things, for then we would be making mental prayer a matter of technique. Basically one can practice mental prayer any time, anywhere, and in a wide variety of physical attitudes, in the holy freedom of God's children. Still, we are not pure spirit but creatures of spirit and body, and we need to learn how to use space and time in the service of the spirit; all the more so because our minds sometimes are incapable of praying. Then we are fortunate to have "brother donkey," as St. Francis of Assisi called the body, come to our aid and in some manner, make up for our inability by a sign of the cross, a prostration, or the movements of rosary beads through our fingers.

1. *Time*

WHEN TO DO MENTAL PRAYER   All times are good for praying, but one should try as far as possible to pray at the most favorable time—when the mind is relatively fresh, not yet crowded with pressing concerns, when there will not be constant interruptions, and so on. Realistically, though, we often do not have the option of praying at an ideal time, but must take advantage of the opportunities allowed us by our other commitments.

We also need to profit from the grace that goes with particular circumstances. The time after the Eucharist, for example, is undoubtedly a privileged time for mental prayer.

Here is a point worth underlining: The mental prayer should not be treated as something exceptional, done at a time snatched with difficulty from other activities, but should become a habit, part of the normal rhythm of our lives, so that its place is never questioned, even for a single day. This will foster fidelity to mental prayer, which is essential. Life is shaped by rhythms: the rhythm of heartbeat and breathing, the rhythm of day and night, of meals, of weeks, and so on. Mental prayer should become a daily event as vital to us as the basic rhythms of existence. It should become the breathing of our souls.

HOW LONG MENTAL PRAYER SHOULD LAST   The time spent in prayer should be adequate. Five minutes are not enough for God. Five minutes are what we give someone when we want to get rid of him or her. A quarter of an hour is the absolute minimum, and anyone who is able should not hesitate to spend an hour on prayer, or even more, every day.

Sometimes, though, one must be careful not to be

overly ambitious in deciding how much time to devote to prayer. There is a risk of taking on more than one could handle and end up discouraged. A relatively short time (twenty minutes or half an hour), spent faithfully on mental prayer every day, is better than two hours now and then.

It is very important to fix a minimum length of time for prayer and not shorten it (except in really exceptional circumstances). It would be a mistake to base the decision on the pleasure we take in praying, so that when it begins to get a bit boring, we stop. Sometimes it may indeed be wise to stop, if the attempt to pray is based on fatigue and anxiety. But as a general rule, for mental prayer to bear fruit, we must keep faithfully to a minimum length and not give in to the temptation to shorten it. This is all the more important because experience shows that it is often in the last five minutes that our Lord visits us and blesses us, after we have spent all the rest of the time working "without catching anything," like St. Peter at his fishing.

2. *Place*

God is present everywhere, and we can pray anywhere at all: in our room, in an oratory, before the Blessed Sacrament, on a train or even in a supermarket checkout line. But obviously it is desirable to find a place that favors silence, recollection, and attention to God's presence. The best place of all, when feasible, is a chapel with the

Blessed Sacrament, especially if it is exposed, so that we can benefit from the grace of our Lord's Real Presence.

If mental prayer is done at home, it is a good idea to make a sort of prayer-corner to suit ourselves, with icons, a candle, a little altar, or whatever else helps. We need material things and outward signs. The Word became flesh, after all, and it would be a great mistake to despise material things and use them when they can help devotion. When prayer becomes harder, resting one's eyes on an icon or a candle flame can lead us back to God's presence.

Just as we should have a time for praying, there should also be a place for praying in every home. Many families today feel the need to reserve a room or a corner of a room as a kind of oratory.

3. *Physical attitudes*

The attitude or position we adopt when doing mental prayer is of no great importance in itself. Mental prayer, I repeat, is not yoga. The best attitude depends on individuals, on their state of tiredness or health, and what suits them personally. Mental prayer can be done sitting, kneeling, face down on the floor, or even standing up or lying in bed.

Despite this freedom in principle, though, a couple of points need noting. In the first place, the position chosen should be one that can be held comfortably, so that we can be still, remain recollected, breathe easily, and so forth. If we are so uncomfortable that we have to shift about every few minutes, the awareness of God's presence that is essential to prayer will suffer.

At the same time, the physical attitude should not be too relaxed either. Mental prayer requires turning one's attention to God's presence, and the bodily position should encourage this orienting of the heart to God. Sometimes, when we are tempted to be lazy, a physical attitude that better expresses our search for and desire for God—kneeling on a prie-dieu or kneeler, for instance, with hands open—will enable us to focus on God. It is another case of using "brother donkey" in the service of the spirit.

V Some methods of mental prayer

1. *Preliminary ideas*

Next, in light of what has been said so far, a few thoughts on the main methods of mental prayer. Quite often none is required. But it sometimes helps to be able to fall back on one or another of the methods to be covered here.

First, how do you choose one way of praying over another? We are absolutely free in this matter, and each should choose the method that suits him best, in which he feels at ease and can grow in love for God. Whatever method we employ, we must take pains to remain in the spiritual "climate" or attitude described above. The Holy Spirit will guide us and do the rest.

We also need to persevere. Whichever method we use, there will be times of dryness, and we must avoid the temptation to abandon a way of praying after just a few days because we are not getting the expected results. Yet at the same time we need to be free and detached. Up to now, perhaps, we have prayed in a way we found good and fruitful, but if the Spirit prompts us to leave it because it is time for something else, we should not cling to what we've grown accustomed to.

Finally, several different methods can be "combined," so that, for example, part of our mental prayer is spent on meditation, and part dedicated to the Jesus Prayer. But beware of the danger of flitting from one thing to another. It is not a good idea to switch to a different way of praying every few minutes. Mental prayer should have a certain stillness, a stability enabling it to be a real exchange of love at a deep level. The movements of love are slow and peaceful: they are stable attitudes because they involve the whole of our being in receiving God and giving ourselves.

2. Meditation

As we saw earlier, meditation has been the basis of almost all the methods of mental prayer proposed in the West since at least the sixteenth century.[1] But it goes even further back than that, being rooted in the constant custom of the Church, and in the Jewish tradition that preceded it, of a spiritual, interiorized reading of Scripture that leads to prayer. Monastic *lectio divina* —the reading of Scripture or spiritual books—is one of the most characteristic examples.

Meditation starts with a period of preparation, which may be shorter or longer and may or may not have a

[1] This fact should be borne in mind when reading classical authors like St. Teresa of Avila and St. John of the Cross. Otherwise there is a risk of misunderstanding certain of their teachings, which assume that the person has started along the path of mental prayer through the practice of meditation and which may not be applicable without modification to someone who has entered on the way of mental prayer by another route, as often happens today.

definite structure, by which one places oneself in God's presence, invokes the Holy Spirit, etc. The meditation itself consists of reading a Scripture text or a passage from a spiritual writer slowly, then making some "considerations" about it—trying to understand what God wants to tell us through this text and how to apply it to our lives. These considerations should enlighten our minds and nourish our love so that we can express the feelings to which they give rise and make resolutions as a result.

Thus the purpose of this reading is not to increase intellectual knowledge but love for God. It should not be rushed but should be done slowly, dwelling on each point, "ruminating" on it as long as it provides nourishment for the soul, and turning it into prayer, conversation with God, acts of thanksgiving or adoration. Having, at it were, wrung all the benefit possible from one point, we should go on to the next point or the next passage of the text. Often it is advisable to end with a prayer summing up all we have meditated, thanking our Lord for it, and asking him for the grace to put it into practice.

Many books give methods and themes for this kind of meditation. As an example, see the beautiful letter from Father Libermann to his nephew found in Appendix 1, or the advice given by St. Francis de Sales in his *Introduction to the Devout Life*.

The advantage of meditation resides in its accessibility as a method of starting mental prayer. It is not very difficult to put into practice and avoids the risk of spiritual laziness by involving activity, our thought processes, and our will.

However, it also has certain dangers. It may become more of a mental exercise than a movement of the heart, and we may end up paying more attention to the considerations we make about God than to God himself. The pleasure we take in our own cleverness may cause us to become subtly attached to it as a form of intellectual activity.

Then, too, meditation generally speaking becomes—sooner or later, quite simply impossible. The mind can no longer meditate, read things, and make considerations, etc., in the way just described. But this is normally a good sign.[2] Such dryness often means that God wants to lead the soul into a way of mental prayer that is more stark, but deeper and more passive. As has been explained, this is an indispensable step. Meditation unites us to God by concepts, images, and sense-impressions, but God is beyond all that, and at a certain point we must leave it all behind in order to find God in himself by traveling a way that is poorer but brings our essential selves closer to his Essence.

[2] St. John of the Cross lays down some ways to determine whether incapacity to meditate is really a sign that God wishes to lead a person into deeper contemplative prayer. The dryness could obviously be caused by other things: either lukewarmness, which involves losing a taste for the things of God; or psychological causes—a sort of mental exhaustion that blocks interest in anything whatsoever. If it proceeds from God, this inability to meditate will be accompanied by two things: first, a definite inclination toward silence and solitude, the desire to remain quietly in God's presence; and second, the absence of any desire to apply one's imagination to anything except God (see *The Ascent of Mount Carmel*, chap. 13).

St. John of the Cross's basic lesson is not so much about how to meditate well, but how to leave meditation behind when the time comes without getting upset, welcoming the inability to meditate as a gain instead of a loss.

To sum up, meditation is good insofar as it frees us from attachment to the world, to sin and to lukewarmness, and brings us closer to God. But we need to know how to leave it aside when the time comes—and obviously it is up to God's wisdom and not us, to decide when that is. Note, too, that even if we no longer practice meditation as our habitual form of mental prayer, it can sometimes be good to go back to it. Reading and considerations and a more active search for God can be useful in keeping us from falling into a sort of spiritual laziness or slackness in mental prayer, as can happen. Finally, even if meditation is not, or is no longer, the basis of one's mental prayer, *lectio divina* should have a place in everyone's spiritual life. It is essential to read Scripture or spiritual books frequently, to nourish the mind and heart on the things of God, while being ready to interrupt the reading from time to time so as to pray about points that strike us.

Is meditation really a suitable form of mental prayer for people today? There is no reason why it shouldn't be, provided we can avoid the pitfalls just mentioned, and can draw benefit from it. At the same time, it is undoubtedly true that present-day mindsets and forms of spiritual experience cause many people to feel ill at ease with meditation and more at home with a less systematic but simpler and more immediate sort of mental prayer.

3. *The "Jesus Prayer"*

The Jesus Prayer, or Prayer of the Heart, is the royal way to the life of prayer in the Eastern Christian tradition and especially in Russia. It has become fairly widespread in the West in recent years, and it is good that it has because it can lead many souls to inner prayer.

The Jesus Prayer consists of the repetition of a short formula, such as "Lord Jesus, Son of the Living God, have mercy on me, a sinner!" The formula must contain the name of Jesus, the human name of the Word. This way of praying is linked to a very beautiful "spirituality of the Name" rooted in the Bible. It is a very ancient tradition.

Among many others, St. Macarius of Egypt, who lived in the fourth century, witnesses to it. The most ordinary things were for him signs that led him to raise his eyes to the supernatural. Thus he reminded St. Pemen of a habit of Eastern women:

> When I was a child, I used to see them chewing betel-nuts to sweeten their saliva and remove any bad odor from their mouths. That is what the Name of our Lord Jesus Christ should be for us: if we chew this blessed name by pronouncing it constantly, it brings all sweetness to our souls, and reveals to us heavenly things, through Him who is the food of joy, the well of salvation, the spring of living waters, the

sweetness of all sweetnesses; and all evil thoughts are expelled from the mind by this name, the name of Him who is in the heavens, our Lord Jesus Christ, the King of Kings, the Lord of all lords, heavenly reward for those who seek Him with all their heart.

The advantage of this prayer is that it is poor, simple, and based on an attitude of great humility. It can lead to a deep mystical life of union with God.

It can be used almost anywhere and at any time, even in the midst of other occupations, and so can lead to continual prayer. Usually it becomes simplified with time, becoming no more than the invocation of the Name "Jesus" or something very brief, such as "Jesus, I love you," or "Jesus, mercy," as the Spirit prompts each individual.

Above all—though this is a free gift from God and must never be forced—this prayer "passes down from the mind into the heart." As it grows simpler, it is interiorized so as to become nearly automatic and constant, a kind of perpetual indwelling of the Name of Jesus in one's heart. Bearing this Name within it in love, the heart prays ceaselessly and one makes one's own home there, in the heart, where the name of Jesus dwells—that Name from which flow love and peace. "Your name is perfume poured out" (Song 1: 3).

The Jesus Prayer clearly is an excellent kind of mental prayer, but it is a gift not given to everyone, at least not in the form just described. Yet that is no reason not to pray by keeping the name of Jesus in our hearts and minds as much as possible and repeating often and lovingly. This is a way of being united to God, since the name represents—indeed, makes present—the Person.

The danger of the Jesus Prayer would be to try to force things by attempting a mechanical, tiring repetition of it that would end in nervous tension. It should be prayed in moderation, gently and unforced, without trying to prolong it longer than God grants us and leaving it up to him to transform it into something more interior and continual if he so desires. Recall the principle laid down at the start: deep prayer is not the result of technique, it is a grace.

4. *The Rosary*

Some people may be surprised to find the traditional rosary treated as a method of mental prayer. But the rosary has made prayer that is contemplative, even continual, possible for many people, perhaps without their even realizing it.

The rosary is also a simple, poor prayer, for poor people—and who is not poor? It has the advantage of being a prayer for all seasons: community prayer, family prayer, prayer of petition (when we want to pray for someone, it is natural to say a decade of the rosary for him). But, at least for those who receive the grace, it can also be prayer of the heart that, very much like the Jesus Prayer, leads into mental prayer. After all, the name of Jesus is at the center of the Hail Mary.

In the rosary it is Mary who leads us into her own prayer, gives us access to the humanity of Jesus and introduces us into the mysteries of her Son. Mary somehow offers us a share in her own mental prayer, surely the deepest ever.

Often, when said slowly and in a spirit of recollection, the rosary can establish our hearts in communion with God. Mary's heart gives us access to Jesus' Heart. Finding it difficult to be recollected and do mental prayer, I have many times had the experience of beginning the rosary and quickly reached inner peace and communion with God. Today, after a period of neglect, the rosary is being rediscovered as a very valuable way of entering into the grace of deep, loving prayer. It is not a matter of fashion or a return to an outworn devotion, but a sign of Mary's maternal presence, so very evident in our times. She wishes to lead the hearts of all her children back to their Father through prayer.

5. *How to tackle certain difficulties*

DRYNESS, DISTASTE, TEMPTATIONS   However we do mental prayer, we can be sure of encountering difficulties. Some have already been mentioned: dryness, distaste, a sense of our own worthlessness, the feeling the effort to pray is useless.

The first thing to say about such difficulties is that they should not come as a surprise or cause us to worry or be upset. Not only are they inevitable, they are actually good for us. They purify our love for God and strengthen our faith. They should be received as a grace, for they are part of the teaching method God uses to sanctify us and bring us closer to himself. Our Lord never permits us to experience a time of trial unless he intends it to bring more abundant graces once it is over. Do not be discouraged. Persevere. Our Lord, who sees our good will, will turn everything to our advantage.

What has already been said here should make clear the significance of such difficulties and how to cope with them.

As for major, persistent difficulties that rob us of our peace of mind—a total, lasting inability to pray, which can sometimes happen—one should open one's heart to a spiritual director who offers reassurance and gives appropriate advice.

DISTRACTIONS   Distractions are one of the more common difficulties in prayer. They are absolutely normal and should neither surprise nor sadden us. When we realize that we have become distracted from our prayer and our thoughts are wandering, rather than getting discouraged or angry, we should simply, peacefully and gently bring our minds back to God. If a period of mental prayer consisted of nothing but this, constantly straying and constantly returning to our Lord, it wouldn't matter. For in constantly struggling to return to the Lord, our prayer, however poor, will be very pleasing to God. He is a Father. He knows what we are made of. He does not require success but good will. It is often much better to learn to accept one's poverty and powerlessness without becoming discouraged or saddened by it, than to do everything perfectly.

Recall, too, that apart from certain exceptional states brought about by God himself, it is absolutely impossible to control and fix the activity of the human mind completely, so that it is totally recollected and attentive without any straying or distraction. Mental prayer presupposes recollection, but it is not a technique of mental concentration. Trying to achieve absolute recollection would be a mistake that would produce nervous tension more than anything else.

Even in the more passive states of prayer, there is still a certain amount of activity of the mind, thoughts, and imagination. The heart is in an attitude of peaceful recollection, of deep orientation toward God, but our thoughts continue to wander to some extent. A nuisance perhaps, but not serious, and it does not prevent the heart's union with God. Those tiny, buzzing flies—our wayward thoughts —do not interrupt the recollection of the heart.

When prayer is still very "cerebral," mainly the activity of the mind, distractions are annoying, because then we are no longer praying. But if we have entered by God's grace into a deeper kind of prayer, a prayer of the heart, distractions are less annoying. The thoughts will usually still keep coming and going, but that will not prevent the heart from praying.

The proper response to distractions, then, is not for the mind to concentrate harder but for the heart to love more intensely.

*

I have said many things, and very little. May this book help some people set out on the way of mental prayer or be encouraged to persevere. That is my only aim in writing. If the reader, with a bit of good will, puts into practice what I have tried to say, the Holy Spirit will do the rest.

For those who wish to go into the subject more deeply, I recommend the writings of the saints, especially those referred to in these pages. That is where to find the deepest teachings and those least likely to become obsolete. Too many books containing wonderful treasures, of enormous potential use to ordinary Christians, are left to gather dust on library shelves. If the masters of Christian spirituality were better known, fewer young people would feel the need to turn to "gurus" to quench their thirst for spiritual things.

APPENDICES

I.

Method of meditation
proposed by Father Liebermann.[1]

Letter to his fifteen-year-old nephew François
to teach him how to do mental prayer.[2]

I bless God for the good desires he gives you, and I can
only encourage you to apply yourself to mental prayer.
Here, more or less, is a method you can follow in order to
acquire the habit of it. First, the evening before, read from
a good book about some devout topic, whatever is best
suited to your taste and your needs. It may be, for example, on how to practice the virtues, or especially on the
life and example of our Lord Jesus Christ or the Blessed
Virgin Mary. At night, think of these good things as you
go to sleep, and in the morning, as you get up, recall the
pious reflections that will form the subject of your prayer.
After your vocal prayer, place yourself in God's presence.
Think that this great God of ours is everywhere, that he is

[1] Venerable Francis Liebermann (1802–1852) was one of the founders of
the Congregation of the Holy Spirit (Holy Ghost Fathers), a missionary order.

[2] *Lettres du Vénérable Père Liebermann présentées par L. Vogel* (Paris: Desclée de
Brouwer, 1964).

.

in the place where you are; that in a very special way he is in your own heart, and adore him. Then think about yourself, and how unworthy you are because of your sins to come before his infinite Holiness and Majesty. Humbly ask his forgiveness for your faults, make an act of contrition and say the Confiteor. Then recognize that of yourself you are incapable of praying to God as you should, and invoke the Holy Spirit, imploring him to come to your aid, teach you how to pray and enable you to do your mental prayer well; say the prayer "Come, Holy Spirit." [3] Then your actual mental prayer will begin. It contains three points, viz.: adoration; consideration; resolution.

1ST—ADORATION Begin by paying homage to God or to our Lord Jesus Christ or the Blessed Virgin Mary, depending on the subject of your meditation. Thus, for example, if you are meditating on one of God's perfections or on a virtue, you will pay homage to God who possesses that perfection to an infinitely high degree, or to our Lord who practiced that virtue so perfectly. For instance, if you are doing your prayer on humility, you will think how humble our Lord was, he who was God from all eternity and lowered himself to become a baby, to be born in a stable, to be obedient to Mary and Joseph for so many years, to wash his Apostles' feet, to suffer all sorts of insults

[3] Come Holy Spirit, fill the hearts of Your faithful and enkindle in them the fire of Your love. Send forth Your spirit, and they shall be created. And You shall renew the face of the earth.

and ignominy from men. Then you will express to him your wonder, your love, your gratitude, and stir up your heart to love him and desire to imitate him.

You can equally consider this virtue in the life of our Lady or even of another Saint; see how they practiced it, and express to our Lord your desire to imitate them.

If you are meditating on one of the mysteries of our Lord, for example the mystery of Christmas, you can picture to yourself the spot where the mystery took place, and the people there; you can imagine the manger where the Savior was born, picture the divine Baby Jesus in Mary's arms, with St. Joseph beside them; the shepherds and the Magi who come to pay him their homage, and then unite yourself to them to adore him, praise him and pray to him. You can also make use of that kind of representation if you are meditating on the great truths such as hell, judgment, or death; for example, picture yourself at the moment of death, with the people who may be around you: a priest, your relatives; imagine the feelings you will have then; and produce the acts of love for God, and the feelings of fear and of trust, that you will have then. After you have paused over these affections and feelings for as long as you find substance in them to occupy yourself usefully, you will then go on to the second point, consideration.

2ND—CONSIDERATION   Here, you will gently turn over in your mind the main reasons which should convince you of the truth which you are meditating on, for example, of the need to work for your salvation, if is it salvation on which you are meditating; or the reasons which should move you to practice this or that virtue. For instance, if you are doing your prayer on humility, you could consider the many reasons for you to be humble: first, the example of our Lord and that of our Lady and all the Saints; then, because pride is the source and cause of all sins, while humility is the foundation for all virtues; and lastly, because you have nothing from which you can draw vanity. What do you have which you have not received from God? Your life, your preservation, your health of mind, your holy thoughts: everything comes from God, so that you have nothing to pride yourself on. Just the contrary, you have much about which to humble yourself, on thinking of how often you have offended your God, your Savior, your Benefactor.

For these considerations, do not attempt to call to mind *all* the reasons that there may be to convince yourself of this or that truth, or to practice this particular virtue, but simply dwell on those which most apply to you or which will most strongly induce you to practice the virtue. Do this consideration gently, without exhausting your mind. When one consideration no longer makes an impression on you, go on to another. Combine all this with acts of devotion towards our Lord and desires of pleasing him; make short prayers and aspirations to him from time to time, to express to him your heart's good desires.

After having considered these reasons, you will turn to the depths of your conscience and examine carefully to see how you have behaved so far with regard to the truth or the virtue on which you have meditated; what faults you have committed, for example, against humility, if it is humility you are meditating on; in what circumstances you committed those faults, and what measures you could take so as not to fall into them again. And then you will go on to the third point, resolutions.

3RD—RESOLUTIONS   One of the best fruits you should take from your mental prayer is making good resolutions. Remember that you should not simply say, "I will not be proud any more," or "I will not say anything in praise of myself," or "I will not be bad-tempered any more," or "I will practice charity towards everyone," etc. These are undoubtedly good desires, which show a good disposition of the soul. But you need to go further: you need to ask yourself in which circumstances of your day you will risk falling into the fault you wish to avoid, or in which circumstances you will be able to make an act of this particular virtue. For example, let us suppose you meditated on humility: and then, when you looked at yourself closely, you noticed that when the teacher asks you a question in class, you feel within yourself a great sense of pride, a keen desire to be admired. So your resolution will be to recollect yourself for an instant when you are asked a question, to make an inner act of humility, to tell God that you renounce with all your heart all the feelings of pride which could arise in your soul. If you have noticed that you are a little dissipated in certain circumstances, your resolution will be either to avoid those circumstances if you can, or to recollect yourself a little just when you foresee that dissipation may occur. If you have noticed that you feel a slight repugnance for a particular person, you will make the resolution to go out towards them and show them real friendship. And so on and so forth.

But, however much you make excellent resolutions, it will all serve for nothing unless God comes to your help. Therefore take good care to ask him insistently for his grace. Do this after making your resolutions and while making them, asking him to keep you faithful to them. But also do it from time to time at other stages of your mental prayer. Generally speaking, your meditation should not be dry, a mere work of your own mind: your heart should expand and pour itself out before your good Master, like the heart of a child before a father who loves him tenderly. To make these petitions more fervent and more effective, you can tell God lovingly that it is for his glory that you are asking for the grace to practice the virtue you have been meditating on; it is to fulfill his holy will, as the Angels do in heaven, that you are asking him for help to be faithful to your good resolutions; that you are asking it in the name of his dear Son Jesus Christ, who died on the Cross to merit all these graces for you; and that he has promised to respond to those who pray to him every time they pray in the name of his Son.

Commend yourself sincerely to the Blessed Virgin Mary too. Beseech our good Mother to intercede for you. She is all-powerful, and all goodness; she does not know how to refuse us, and God our Lord grants her everything she asks for us. Pray also to your patron saint and your guardian angel. Their prayers cannot fail to obtain for you the grace, the virtue, the faithfulness to your resolutions, which you need.

From time to time in the course of the day you will recall your good resolutions so as to put them into practice, or to check whether you have kept them, and renew them for the remainder of the day. From time to time, you will lift up your heart to our Lord, asking him to revive in you the good dispositions he sent you during your morning prayer. By acting in this way, be sure that you will profit greatly from this holy exercise, and that you will make great progress in virtue and in the love of God.

As for distractions in your prayers, do not be too concerned about them. As soon as you notice them, reject them, and continue peacefully with your mental or vocal prayers. It is impossible for us never to have any distractions; all that our good Lord asks of us is that we should be faithful in returning to him as soon as we notice that we have been distracted from him. Little by little, these distractions will diminish, and prayer will become sweeter and easier to you.

These, my dear nephew, are the instructions which I think will facilitate for you the practice of mental prayer, which is so necessary. Mental prayer is the great means which all the saints have employed in order to reach holiness. I hope that by God's grace, it will profit you as it did them, and that this good Master of ours will reward your good will by his graces.

— • —

2.

The Practice of the Presence of God [3]

According to Brother Lawrence of the Resurrection (1614–1691)

The practice which is most holy and necessary in the spiritual life is the practice of the presence of God. It consists of taking pleasure in and becoming accustomed to his divine company, speaking humbly with him and conversing lovingly with him at all times, at every moment, without any rules but without measure; especially in times of temptations, sufferings, aridities, revulsion, and even infidelities and sins.

We should continually strive to ensure that all our actions are like little conversations with God, quite un-

[3] Extract from Brother Lawrence of the Resurrection, *L'Expérience de la présence de Dieu* (Paris: Le Seuil, 1998).

studied, just using the words that come from the purity and simplicity of the heart.

We should perform all our actions with due weight and measure, without being impetuous or hasty, for that would indicate a distracted mind. We should work with God, calmly and lovingly, begging him to accept our work, and by that continual attention to God, we will crush the devil's head and make his weapons fall from his hands.

During our work and other activities, during our reading—even our spiritual reading—and during our outward devotions and vocal prayers, we should stop for a brief instant as often as we can to adore God in the depths of our heart, taste his sweetness momentarily and, catching him as it were by surprise, praise him, ask him for help, offer him our heart, and thank him.

What can be more pleasing to God than for us to leave created things aside a thousand times every day in order to turn to him and adore him within us?

We cannot give God greater proof of our fidelity than by renouncing and despising created things over and over again, to enjoy the Creator for just a single moment. Little by little, that exercise destroys the pride which can only continue to exist amidst creatures, and our frequent turnings to God progressively set us free from creatures.

It is not necessary to be always in church in order to be with God. We can make our heart into an oratory, into which we withdraw from time to time, to spend time talking with him. Everyone is capable of these friendly conversations with God; a little lifting up of the heart is enough, a little recollection of God, an act of inner adoration, even when you are running, sword in hand. These are prayers which, however brief, are nevertheless very pleasing to God, and which, far from making one lose one's courage amidst very dangerous occasions, actually strengthen it. Remember to do this, then, as much as you can; this way of praying is very appropriate and most necessary to a soldier, who is exposed to deadly dangers every day, and often to dangers for his eternal salvation.

This practice of the presence of God is of great help in doing mental prayer well; for, by preventing the mind from wandering during the day, and by holding it close to God, it makes it easier for it to remain quiet during mental prayer.

— • —